03/08/2071

NARROW
GAUGE
ALBUM
1965-1985
IN COLOUR

Linda, now on the Festiniog Railway in 'as received from Penrhyn' condition, coupled to tender No. 38 with Allan Garraway driving, shunting her train at Portmadoc at the north end of the Cob. Note carriage No. 12 is now converted into a buffet car.

[PREVIOUS PAGE] A tall old Festiniog Railway company signal stands proud protecting Stesion Fein on 11th April 1971.

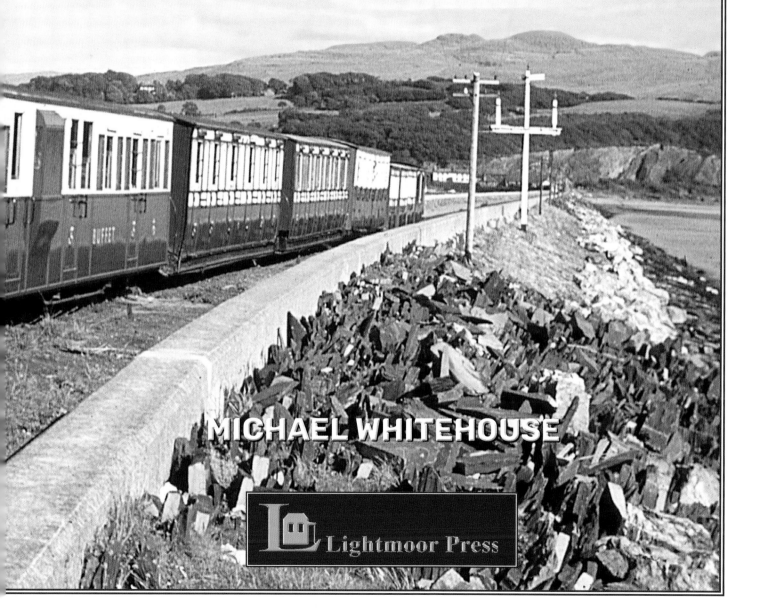

NARROW GAUGE ALBUM

1965-1985
IN COLOUR

MICHAEL WHITEHOUSE

Lightmoor Press

The site of Stesion Fein on The Festiniog Railway 11th April, 1971, connecting with the former L&NWR main line at Blaenau Ffestiniog, with the water tower still standing together with the original station track formation as far as the new road bisecting the railway.

ACKNOWLEDGEMENTS

Most of the pictures in this book are from my own collection. Where these have been taken by other people they are acknowledged by initials: Pat Whitehouse [PBW], Eric Russell [ESR] and Ken Cooper [KC]. I have also been fortunate to be offered pictures taken by others and, where known, these are fully credited.

Several friends have helped me with research, text and images seeking to ensure facts are correct, but all mistakes are my responsibility.

I would like to thank my mother who has enjoyed checking the text and recalling some of the stories first hand, especially of course the Talyllyn, where we spent many holidays, and reminiscing about many of the people mentioned in this book. I have also received help from John Dobson, Martin Fuller, Bob Harris, Ann Hatherill, John Heys, Peter Lemmey, Emily Mead, David Mitchell and Will Smith.

The observant reader will notice that the railway and place name spellings vary throughout the text. This is deliberate. Names change over time for many reasons, so I have used the relevant spelling for the time, even if that changes within an individual essay; everything evolves. Portmadoc, for instance, became Porthmadog in 1974.

ABOUT THE AUTHOR

Michael Whitehouse has always been interested in narrow gauge railways, at home and abroad. In his childhood, he was largely brought up on the Talyllyn Railway in the 1950s when his father, 'PBW', was Secretary of the preservation society and family holidays were nearly always in Wales. As soon as he was able to volunteer in university holidays, he worked on the Festiniog Railway at Boston Lodge Works and occasionally fired the summer high season trains. Later, he became a qualified fireman on the Welshpool & Llanfair Railway. He is a commercial lawyer by profession and has advised on many complex railway projects in Britain, Africa and Asia. In his legal capacity he volunteered to assist the regeneration of the Welsh Highland Railway by the Festiniog Railway; he joined the core reconstruction team and assisted with negotiations and settling contracts, became Chairman of the construction company and later of the Festiniog Railway Company itself.

CONTENTS

Published by
LIGHTMOOR PRESS
© Lightmoor Press & Michael Whitehouse 2019
Designed by Neil Parkhouse

British Library Cataloguing-in-Publication Data.
A catalogue record for this book is available from the British Library

ISBN: 9781911038 69 6

LIGHTMOOR PRESS
Unit 144B, Harbour Road Trading Estate, Lydney, Gloucestershire GL15 4EJ
www.lightmoor.co.uk / info@lightmoor.co.uk

Lightmoor Press is an imprint of Black Dwarf Lightmoor Publications Ltd

Printed in Poland
www.lfbookservices.co.uk

The Snowdon Mountain Railway was built specifically to take tourists to a sometimes dangerous but much sought after inaccessible place, now designated as having the best view in the United Kingdom: the summit of Wales' highest mountain. The SMR has always been run as a commercial concern and, apart from times of war, has consistently turned in increasing traffic figures. Here we see a train powered by one of the later series rack locomotives in April 1979 near Llanberis on the most level section of the railway, albeit still at an incline of 1 in 50.

Appropriately named *The Eclipse*, a Bagnall steam locomotive converted in 1927 to run on electricity by collecting current from overhead trolley wires, worked on level 7 to the slate tips at Llechwedd Quarry in Blaenau Ffestiniog. This quarry opened in the late 1840s and connected to the Festiniog Railway in 1854. Progressive management looked forwards: tourists were encouraged to visit the underground workings by means of a new rail system from 1976, the use of rail for slate transport was eliminated by 1981 and, more recently, the quarry management has moved into adventure tourism, always keeping ahead. *The Eclipse* is seen here abandoned but still in its correct setting in October 1979.

INTRODUCTION

Narrow Gauge Railways 1950-65 In Colour, published in 2018, portrayed the narrow gauge scene in the British Isles during the survival years following the Second World War. Many such lines were either on their last legs, had already closed or were about to. The passenger narrow gauge lines in Ireland had all gone by the 1960s and those in Scotland has perished before the war. Preservation, in the form of voluntary run railways, was in its infancy. The Talyllyn was the first, followed closely by the Festiniog Railway, although the majority of the survivors were still commercially run: The Snowdon Mountain, Vale of Rheidol and Isle of Man as examples.

This book covers the changing years of the narrow gauge and so is a sequel. In Wales, a metamorphosis was underway. Narrow gauge lines were being exhumed or improved to carry an increasing number of tourists. In England, there remained a few industrial concerns, such as the sand line in Leighton Buzzard, which either bequeathed their steam locomotives or provided access to preservationists. Whilst these days we refer to the preservation movement, this was in all reality in its infancy until the 1960s. In order for these narrow gauge lines to survive at all and then move forward to enter the tourist industry and be accepted as economic generators, they had to change, sometimes rapidly and often without much thought to past heritage; that would come later. So, in this book, we will chart their progress as the railways hastened to get themselves fit enough to carry larger numbers of passengers than had perhaps been dreamed of.

In 1978, my father, Pat Whitehouse, John Snell, both amongst the first volunteers on a preserved railway, and Brian Hollingsworth, a professional civil engineer, wrote a book called *Steam for Pleasure*. Their words below set the scene:

'A hundred years or so ago, there were few steam railways run solely for pleasure. Narrow gauge trains took tourists to beauty spots but, apart from a very few instances, nowhere were the trains themselves the main attraction. It was the advent of road transport, more pliant and convenient that, by causing the demise of many minor lines, with their previously unappreciated charm, eventually led people to consider railway preservation as an activity worthwhile in itself.

Nostalgia for the past and a desire to preserve it led to the invention of voluntarily run railways to deliver the dream. But some dreams were initially too unrealistic in the immediate post war years. Many enthusiasts wandered the abandoned and forlorn trackbed of the Welsh Highland Railway, particularly the section south of Snowdon by the enchanting village of Beddgelert, nestling just above the narrow defile of the Aberglaslyn Pass which led the way to the sea. Here we see Beddgelert station on 10th June 1965, abandoned with just the concrete pillars of the water tank and associated pit between the rails remaining. Even these were scheduled to be demolished by the new station construction plan devised during the 21st century rebuilding but, fortuitously, nostalgia won the day and the water tank is now restored and functional and has even filled the tanks of the North Wales Narrow Gauge Railway's original 2-6-2T *Russell*, so creating more dreams to taunt enthusiasts to deliver in the future. [KC]

The railways that disappeared often served remote and beautiful countryside, and their trains, because of dire poverty, were quaint and delightful. They possessed an individuality, and so their abandonment caused a sense of almost personal loss.

It was the impending closure, in 1950, of what was then the oldest working steam hauled narrow gauge railway, the Talyllyn, which gave rise to a movement which has now spread the world over. Wales has been the home of many narrow gauge systems, mostly constructed for the carriage of slate from the mountains to the coast, but which, as affluence arrived and paid holidays became the vogue, carried a not insubstantial tourist traffic during the summer months.

As the preservation movement gathered force it rapidly became apparent that volunteer labour and enthusiasm, though vital in their own way, were not enough. Something which began as an evocative and emotional hobby needed to be developed into a leisure industry with a firm business like approach to both management and finance. It is one thing to wish to preserve or perpetuate part of the country's heritage, but quite another to cope adequately with the million or so passenger journeys made over the tracks of what are now the 'Great Little Trains of Wales.'

A great asset is that all the 'Great Little Trains' were built as narrow gauge lines, thus limiting the monetary outlay required for replacements and renewals. Also, their total independence led them to construct their own workshops: the Talyllyn was so equipped to a small degree, in keeping with its rustic atmosphere, and the Festiniog had shops capable of constructing its own locomotives, a fitting situation for the premier narrow gauge line in the kingdom. Because of their uniqueness, narrow gauge and geographical situation, the privately owned lines have been able not only to survive under new ownership as tourist concerns, but also to grow and prosper. Each of the railways has its own peculiar character relative to its terrain, locomotive power and basis of its tourist or preservation ownership. Some are society controlled, others company controlled under trust arrangements, and others purely commercial.'

This colour photograph album takes the narrow gauge story in Britain largely from the 1960s up towards the 1990s. The thirty year period from the 1960s saw the development of the surviving narrow gauge lines in Wales, the establishment of some new tourist lines in England and the preservation of many narrow gauge locomotives by individuals, clubs and museums. The early pictures included here were taken at a time when colour photography was uncommon, largely due to the cost of film. For example, John Dobson, who contributes several images for the essay about *Linda* in 1962-63 reminds us that *'up until 1964 I was still a student and, whilst I had a good camera, colour film was expensive, Kodachrome cost 37s 6d for a 36 exposure cassette, about £41 in today's money, so I usually had to make two cassettes last all summer!'.* But the later images move into a time when colour slide film became generally affordable and was well used, resulting in narrow gauge images proliferating quite widely. The images and their accompanying stories show how the lines which feature survived, adapted and developed in this period.

The 1960s to the early 1990s were very different times to the immediate post-war period, when the nation was then recovering from a second terrible war. By the early 1960s, the country had largely revived and was moving ahead quickly on several fronts. In a massive triumph for Harold Macmillan, the Conservative party won the general election in 1959 with the slogan 'You've never had it so good', reflecting the growing affluence of the electorate. We won the football World Cup in 1966. Concorde, the world's first supersonic airliner, took to the skies in 1969. The UK joined the European Union in 1973. Tim Berners-Lee invented the World Wide Web in 1989. We had, by then, experienced three terms of office by the first ever lady Prime Minister, Margaret Thatcher, who had embarked on a radical programme of

The Isle of Man Railway system was leased for a few years in the mid 1960s by the Marquess of Ailsa and run largely as a dream rather than with a sound business plan. Here we see the former County Donegal twin railcar set and large boilered No. 10 *G.H. Wood* cross at Colby on the Peel line on 22nd July 1968. The Marquess re-opened all three of the Island's lines with panache but gradually retreated just to run the line to Port Erin before admitting defeat.

privatisation, deregulation, trade union reform and tax cuts.

In the railway world, ground breaking changes were also occurring. Railway lines were closing wholesale as a result of the Beeching Report. In 1968, British Railways finally threw the fire out in their last standard gauge steam locomotive but, as we will read later, were obliged to keep operating three narrow gauge ones for longer than they wished. Meanwhile, all manner of quarries and industrial concerns were shutting up shop and making their eclectic collection of steam locomotives redundant; very many were snapped up by enthusiasts for a song. Railway preservation went from strength to strength with many narrow gauge lines being saved from destruction and others rebuilt and extended. There seemed nothing that railway preservationists could not do.

Fortunately too, in this period, the nation became more prosperous overall. Many people owned motor cars and had more holiday time. Young students benefitted from long summer holidays and were enticed to offer their time freely to narrow gauge railways in return for excitement, satisfaction for their contribution and an opportunity to develop friendships with like minded people. Motorways were created and, by 1960, the M1 was punched through the Midlands and the developing network encouraged a major rise in long distance private travel by road. No longer was it necessary for members of the Festiniog Railway London Area Group to drive to North Wales all through the night on Fridays and Sundays to spend a couple of days reviving their favourite railway. Students also had more time and money

as the Robbins Report on Higher Education in 1963 was followed by state paid fees and maintenance grants.

Whilst all this helped generate volunteer support to create and grow tourist railways, soon the enormous growth in ridership would be curbed. Once jet aircraft were introduced into passenger service, holiday companies like Horizon and Thomas Cook began to promote charter flights to foreign lands for sun seekers. Visitors to Wales and the Isle of Man, previously hot spots for the summer factory fortnight, dropped rapidly. Timing could not have been worse for those railways which had built extensions and geared up for three train a day services in the peak season. Railways found it difficult to make ends meet. The Festiniog Railway incurred high borrowings which were not paid off for some twenty years. The private operator of the Isle of Man Railway threw in the towel and handed back his lease; well, just perhaps, he had pushed the boat out a little too much anyway.

With narrow gauge industrial lines closing everywhere, suddenly there were a very large number of delightful and affordable steam locomotives available which would otherwise simply go for scrap. Individuals, some with rose tinted glasses, acquired many of these for a song. Bernard Latham collected quite a few and why not? He visited the Rugby Portland Cement Company to buy his first one: '*Not being an engineer I might as well have picked one out with a pin. I decided that* Triassic *was the most suitable, partly because it had on its side a plate reading* 'Rebuilt 1951' *and partly because it looked to have been the last of the quartet in use.*' He had it transported to live in his garden.

In the 1960s, the Festiniog Railway experienced a high growth in tourist traffic simultaneously with a bad turn for the worse in the reliability of its original locomotive fleet. There was no option but to look elsewhere for motive power. As luck would have it, the nearby Penrhyn Railway was about to close and so could spare *Linda*, one of its 'main line' locomotives, to help out, fortuitously being of the same gauge, or so everyone thought until 5th September, 1962. Here we see *Linda* being craned onto a standard gauge wagon for transport to the FR's exchange yard at Minfford on 13th July; her back-heaviness is self evident, as is the closeness of the front lifting chains to the curved ends of her buffer beam! She was in steam and running up the FR on test two days later. [John Dobson]

Companies were pretty much willing to give their redundant locomotives and stock away. The Talyllyn Railway were pretty quick off the mark in also becoming the home for what is now a very significant collection of narrow gauge items. This lead to the formation of the Narrow Gauge Railway Museum Trust and the establishment of a museum at Towyn Wharf, first of all in the old gunpowder shed, housing *George Henry*, a de Winton vertical boilered locomotive from the Penrhyn Railway. This was soon followed by *Russell*, which had survived the war-time scrap drive on the Welsh Highland Railway and was purchased by the Birmingham Locomotive Club when it also acquired *Secundus* from Purbeck. Hot on its heels came a squat 0-4-0T gifted from the Dublin Guinness brewery. Almost a waterfall of exhibits followed, necessitating the establishment of a new museum building which is now incorporated, to great effect, in the new station at Wharf. The National Trust's Penrhyn Castle Museum also became a haven for narrow gauge relics, many naturally coming from the Penrhyn Railway itself. The Douglas-Pennant family, who lived in the Castle and owned the quarry and the railway, must have been a little bemused that there was so much interest in their locomotives but they readily agreed to some being preserved. The Dinorwic workshop at Llanberis was preserved in its entirety, a complete timewarp, including patterns and even chalk sketches and calculations on blackboards. Many other quarry and industrial locomotives found homes on estates and in gardens. Alan Bloom set up a Nursery Railway round his commercial plant gardens and the Reverend Teddy Boston encircled his rectory with a 2ft gauge railway.

So enjoy the images in this book with their accompanying essays. You will read about the success of dreams once thought impossible and see locomotives of many types, sizes, shapes and colour: double engines, single engines, vertical boilered locomotives, sentinels, Swiss rack locomotives, Simplex diesels and the last British Railways steam locomotives in blue, sporting the controversial white double arrow logo.

The preservation of the Talyllyn Railway in 1950 started it all and many have happily followed suit. My father's words probably sum up what everyone felt in keeping narrow gauge railways and locomotives alive:

'It was a feeling of adventure. It was a challenge. All of us were looking for some kind of challenge because, for years and years and years, we'd been channelled into doing things, particularly those of us who were in the services, rather than being in a situation of accepting a challenge on our own initiative. I think the motivation for all of us was the sense of adventure and of actually being able to do something with a railway of our own.'

Michael Whitehouse
Worcestershire, 2019

In the 1950s and early '60s, industrial concerns were closing and had no further use for their diminutive steam locomotives. Most firms were only too happy to co-operate, enabling enthusiasts to acquire them for display and use. This yellow German 0-4-0WT, built by Freudenstien, worked at ARC's stone quarries in Newlyn, the most westerly railway in Cornwall. It was built in 1900, named *Penlee* in 1910, withdrawn in 1946 and left abandoned but painted up on the quayside, where it is seen here on 20th June 1967; it was rescued for preservation at the Leighton Buzzard Narrow Gauge Railway. [KC]

The original Festiniog Railway Company main line above Dduallt slumbers in April 1970, never to be used for passenger services again. Due to the pumped storage hydroelectric scheme at Tanygrisiau, the Festiniog Railway lost its original trackbed between Moelwyn Tunnel and Tanygrisiau station. But the company fought the longest battle in legal history, eventually winning compensation to help build a new line the hard way, with picks, shovels and wheelbarrows, to join the revived section to Dduallt with the severed section back to Blaenau Ffestiniog.

The antiquated workshop at Pendre on the Talyllyn Railway with one of its original two locomotives being rebuilt, No. 1 *Talyllyn*, an 0-4-2T built by Fletcher, Jennings & Co. of Whitehaven for the line's opening in 1865. When the line was taken over by preservationists in 1951, *Talyllyn* was long past any possibility of working again and so was shunted out to grass in a barn to provide chickens a place to nest. Eric Gibbons, one of the TRPS Council members, offered to rebuild her at no cost to the railway and so, in 1957, *Talyllyn* returned to the line gleaming in green paint and shining brasswork but proved to be a shy steamer. It took the railway's Chief Engineer, John Bate, to fix the problems by a further complete rebuild but now, thankfully and appropriately, No. 1 *Talyllyn* is a reliable locomotive once again.

1
ADAPTING THE TALYLLYN RAILWAY TO THE 20TH CENTURY

Lines of Character. **In a timeless scene, No. 1** *Talyllyn* **lifts the original train up the steepest section on the line out of Rhydyronen station in high summer 1966.** *'The very essence of the Talyllyn Railway was its complete indifference to time.'* **(Allan Garraway).**

By all economic indicators, the Talyllyn Railway should have closed forever by 1910. But it is still very much with us, largely due to two phenomena. First, the philanthropy of Sir Haydn Jones who was also intent on securing his own position as local MP and, second, the emergence of voluntary run railways after the second world war. Neither of these arose for economic reasons, but rather to keep the otherwise quite unremarkable slate carrying narrow gauge mineral railway open for local community benefit and also for its own sake.

Sir Haydn Jones, Liberal member of Parliament for Merioneth and a staunch Methodist, liked to be a figurehead for his constituents and had vowed to keep the Talyllyn Railway, which he bought in 1911, going for the rest of his lifetime. The railway was conceived in the middle of the 19th century to carry slate from the Bryn Eglwys quarries down to the sea at Aberdovey harbour. It was actually only built to the small town of Towyn, some three miles north of Aberdovey

as, by then, the Cambrian standard gauge railway had been constructed along the coast making it unnecessary to take the 2ft 3ins gauge line any further. Slate transshipment was arranged at Kings' Wharf whilst the workshops and passenger station were at the first station up the line at Pendre, on the other side of Towyn itself. Perhaps this solution kept the railway out of sight and mind as far as the Mandarins of Whitehall were concerned when they effected various railway amalgamations and Nationalisation over the years. Anyway, the Talyllyn Railway continued in being, almost in aspic, fulfilling its slate carrying purpose until, in all reality, the amount remaining for commercial exploitation gave out by 1910. Sir Haydn bought the railway mainly to continue to provide some work for the local population but spent as little as possible on the railway's upkeep for forty years. It remained, quite remarkably, almost as built when he died in 1950. That should then have been that.

Slate traffic in the first half of the 20th century was small,

Eating an ice cream at Wharf on 22nd July 1961. The original station at Towyn was laid out for slate traffic and the increased tourist traffic required a new platform at a proper height, with trains departing from the right hand side. Although the original track shown on the left hand side was retained, this was rarely used as the trains could not load passengers at the new platform. This is because the carriages, highly unusually, only have doors on their left hand side following Captain Tyler's 1866 instruction, after he found insufficient clearances under the bridges, requiring the track to be slewed and doors on the right hand side of the carriages to be removed. The slate building in the background is the former gunpowder shed, which was converted to be the original museum housing the De Winton *George Henry* rescued from Penrhyn Quarry. [KC]

Awaiting departure. Children patiently wait at Abergynolwyn for the train to leave for the return journey to the coast on 26th July 1958. The slate station building offers no passenger amenities except rudimentary shelter. The former Penrhyn Railway quarrymens' coaches do not even offer that. [KC]

but the railway had attracted a number of summer tourists who were faithful to the TR as they took their summer holidays in the area each year. The 1920s saw an increase in summer passengers as Britain recovered from the First World War. The four carriages were not enough to carry the traffic on offer and so holidaymakers often enjoyed a trip in the slate wagons fitted with planks as seats! Writer Tom Rolt stumbled across the railway after the Second World War which, luckily, proved to be just at the right time. He even saw what is believed to be the very last wagon loaded with slate sent down the quarry inclines. With the help of his friend Bill Trinder, they were able to have conversations with Sir Haydn about saving the railway just before he died in 1950. This gave them the encouragement they needed to call the inaugural meeting of the nascent Talyllyn Railway Preservation Society in Birmingham which, fortunately, was attended by enough of the right sort of people to get something done. And the timing was good as Britain was slowly beginning to return to normal after a second terrible war fought to secure freedom for individuals and nations. People were beginning to have some spare time and wanted to do something different in a period when the new Labour Government was hell bent on Nationalisation. Rolt inspired the enthusiasts by saying: "*What a fine thing it would be if at least one independent railway could survive to perpetuate the pride and glory of the old companies. Why not the Talyllyn?*" This resulted in a small

group of enthusiasts forming a 'Big Society' and taking over a railway by-way which became their own. Tom had found a ready band of helpers from industry and commerce in the Midlands and North West who lent a hand and ensured their businesses contributed, for they had spent their childhood riding the Talyllyn and had a fondness for it. Between them, they rebuilt the Talyllyn Railway so that many thousands of people could enjoy it.

The preservationists asked for the railway to be given to them and Sir Haydn's widow agreed. The first voluntarily run railway in the world was now a reality. But it all needed rebuilding and replacing to survive. And, bit by bit it was, over the next fifteen years or so. The volunteers set to, ran the railway with enthusiasm and learned much as they went along. As Pat Whitehouse, the Preservation Society's first Secretary put it: "*The motivation for all of us was the sense of adventure and of actually being able to do something with a railway of our own.*" Whitehouse's building firm & carpenters shop and Hunt Bros foundry were both set to work making new things and providing materials for an increasing number of volunteers to rebuild pretty much everything else. Pat Garland, a Birmingham accountant, controlled the finances and eeked out the pounds, shillings and pence day by day to keep the Society solvent. Tom Rolt and his team of volunteers ran the railway from day to day. It was all a gargantuan task, made even more demanding by the railway's luck and

No. 1 *Talyllyn* stands at Wharf with '*The Centenarian*', a new train service introduced for the TR's centenary year in 1965. The lead vehicle in the train is the refreshment van, which was then taken to Abergynolwyn on the first train of the day and returned on the last. The centenary was celebrated on 1st June with John Betjeman as official guest.

Edward Thomas leaves Dolgoch at Easter 1968, running past the new water tank built to accommodate longer trains.

In 1970, No. 2 *Dolgoch* and an ornate bogie carriage, rescued from the nearby Corris Railway, head a train at Towyn Wharf.

Hendy bridge on 18th May 1964, just a little further up the line from the halt of the same name serving a farm. The whole of the Talyllyn Railway had been relaid and its infrastructure completely rebuilt. [KC]

success in attracting more visitors.

To a great extent, the story of holidays and leisure time is intertwined with the fortunes of the Talyllyn and shaped its future development. After the second world war, people had more new-found leisure time and sought to escape the industrial heartlands of both the Midlands and the North West for their holidays. The Welsh coast was reachable and appealing and many people came for their summer holiday 'factory fortnight'. In 1957, the BBC produced a live outside broadcast from the railway and this publicity drew a substantial number of visitors to it, with more than 57,500 in that year alone. Generally, in the latter half of the 1950s and early 1960s, traffic grew to such an extent that more locomotives and carriages were urgently needed to carry the passengers, numbers increasing to some 90,000 holidaymakers by the 1970s. No longer was it satisfactory for three trains to amble up the line three days a week when the only usable steam locomotive was fit enough to work. Now three train sets were required to make some nine or more journeys daily in the summer peak season and run to time to connect with the main line and ensure holidaymakers were back in their boarding houses for high tea.

Merionethshire was booming in the summer holidays. Aberdovey became a centre for water sports and promoted its great expanse of sandy beach. Towyn and the surrounding seaside area in the Cader Idris region sprouted very many caravan parks and all the Mrs Jones and Davies took in

families for bed & breakfast. Most people still came to the coast by train and, in the summer school holidays, it was usual for the Cambrian main line railway to be almost choked with extra trains, many double-headed up the difficult Talerddig Bank over the mountain divide to the Midlands, especially on the routine Saturday change over day.

So, the Talyllyn Railway was rebuilt and adapted to cope with the new heavy traffic demands but it still kept most of its unique quaint character as an independent byway which had escaped the Labour government's Nationalisation policy. Harold Vickers, one of the very early volunteers, puts the problem succinctly: *"We did not expect a financial profit. We just wanted to preserve a working Victorian relic, a museum piece of 1865 vintage. But the task we have set ourselves is an impossible one. The railway of 1856 cannot be kept in working order and fossilised at the same time. If it is to work it must live and if it is to live it must adjust to the circumstances."* And adjust is exactly what the preservationists did. David Leech in describing one of his experiences as a guard says it all really: *"The TR was receiving all the 'operated by volunteers' glory and publicity'. Traffic was growing incredibly. One day, on the last train down, I had twenty-seven passengers in the brake van. On other occasions, after the last arrival of the day at Wharf, the whole train would be propelled back to Dolgoch to pick up the forty or so passengers who had had to wait. It was obvious that the railway had to change to offer the growing number of passengers a safe and acceptable ride."*

No. 4 *Edward Thomas* stands at Pendre repainted in Brunswick green and fitted with a Giesl ejector. Many people thought the GWR painted their locomotives in Brunswick green and, as the 'Birmingham Committee' favoured GWR practice and introduced that company's paint scheme to the TR, a bulk order of Brunswick green was made when engines were due for repainting. Unfortunately, it was then found that GWR locos were painted in deep bronze green but the TR had to use the paint they had bought! Dr Giesl Gieslingen invented his ejector to improve the steaming of Austrian steam locomotives and enable them to burn inferior coal. Somewhat naturally, he sought to expand sales abroad, including to Britain. He discovered that the Earl of Northesk was President of the Talyllyn Railway and as he surely should know the Queen who could instruct British Railways to buy his product, he contacted the Earl on a sales mission. Tom Rolt was interested in improving the line's locomotives and the ejector was fitted to No. 4 rather as a publicity stunt. British Rail hardly bought any Giesl ejectors and even No. 4's wore out after some ten years as it was fabricated from thin steel plate but it can now be seen in the Museum at Towyn Wharf. [KC]

The Talyllyn Railway Preservation Society had begun operating the railway itself on Whit Monday, 14th May 1951. It was then already obvious that all the track, infrastructure, locomotives and carriages were life expired but, somehow and with much effort, the railway continued to be coaxed into life. Opportunities to acquire additional rolling stock were taken up and members' generosity hastily accepted. By the railway's centenary in 1965, it had been largely rebuilt: track relaid, civil engineering improved, the two original Fletcher, Jennings antique locomotives renewed and three additional steam engines procured, two at the eleventh hour from the nearby Corris Railway at Machynlleth, amazingly of the same rare 2ft 3ins gauge as the TR, and one from a Midlands scrap yard originally built for the Royal Air Force. These three 'new' locomotives ran virtually all the traffic in the 1950s, often double-heading long trains. Additional carriages were rescued from abandonment by other closed narrow gauge railways and their purpose turned back to carrying people again instead of being used as greenhouses

or garden sheds. The brothers Green worked wonders with carriage woodwork in the emerging new Pendre workshops as did John Bate who had volunteered to help in the very first year and who became Chief Engineer to orchestrate the upgrading of the Talyllyn to comply with Railway Inspectorate requirements, probably for the first time ever. When the line was originally inspected for opening in 1866, Captain Tyler of the Ministry prescribed a long list of improvements, including slewing the track under bridges, as there was insufficient clearance, requiring all the doors on the southern side of the train to be secured or removed as a result. The track never was slewed and the Ministry seemed to have forgotten about the line over the years. The preservationists bravely (but rightly) invited the Inspectorate to give its considered view of the state and condition of the railway in 1950. By rights, they could have simply closed it down had there been a serious accident but the worst that happened were very many derailments at slow speed. The Railway Inspectorate were sympathetic and, apart from a few sharp

No. 4 *Edward Thomas* takes water at the original slate water tower at Dolgoch station watched by passengers on 26th July 1958. The water source was a mountain stream and whenever the water holding pool in the hillside became blocked with stones or weeds, locomotive crew could often find the tank empty, requiring a quick scramble up to remove the obstructions. No. 4 is one of the two locomotives rescued from the Corris Railway at a price of £25 each. Originally built by Hunslet of Leeds to its standard 'Tatoo' design, the 0-4-2T was bought by the Corris in the 1920s to supplement the original three steam locomotives which had to be cannibalised to keep just one of them working until the line's closure. [KC]

No. 4 *Edward Thomas*, with its original chimney refitted, seen leaving Dolgoch hauling the 19th century four-wheeled carriages at Easter 1969. John Bate, Chief Engineer, reported that the Giesl ejector had been removed as it was simply worn out. He also commented that no significant difference had been noted in No. 4's fuel or water consumption with either chimney but reversion to its original chimney had improved the speed of steam raising. The advantage of the Giesl front end was its ability to allow the locomotive to burn inferior fuel but the TR used only the best South Wales steam coal, so its advantage was minimal.

Celebrating the 21st anniversary of the Talyllyn Railway Preservation Society on 15th May 1976. Chairman James Boyd repeats the formalities of the opening day in 1951, marking the inaugural passenger train operated by the world's first railway preservation society, by cutting the original 1950s white tape once again. On the right hand side of the picture are Dai Jones (driver) and Phil Care (fireman) next to No. 2, with John Slater (Editor of *Talyllyn News*, in a suit). In the foreground taking a picture is President John Adams (with white hair).

comments such as when Brynglas passing loop was installed without prior permission, they seemed to take a benign view, almost on the basis that they accepted the Talyllyn Railway should be kept as an anachronism for enjoyment in the 20th century and, due to the slow speed, little of great harm was likely to transpire. Colonel McMullen did, however, write to say: '*I would remind you that the responsibility for safety of passengers is yours.*'

Over time, as the number of volunteers working on the railway grew, some friction arose between the 'Birmingham Committee' of industrial and commercial volunteers who provided much time, effort and resources but who were not the sort of people 'to take their coats off' themselves, and the hard working volunteers on the ground, who had the daily task of keeping the railway running. The Birmingham Committee simply picked the best of Great Western Railway practice and applied it to the TR, even to the extent of locomotive livery and brass chimney rings. The team on the ground wanted more say. Brian Bushell was brave enough to write to the Council: '*I am convinced that the majority of volunteers at Towyn would be happier to know that their*

money and their affairs were being controlled by people like themselves who had proved their worth at Towyn in recent months; in fact people with whom they might even find themselves working on the trains.'. Council were wise enough to meet Mr Bushell and, whilst the archives contain a copy of a letter written by him to all members declaring that the explanation he was given completely satisfied him and also an unreserved apology for having raised them in the first place, Council duly took note and control of the TRPS moved to Tywyn soon enough. As Pat Whitehouse put it: '*The TR has got to be run by its members and the whole joy of the thing is that is what happens.*'.

The initial Council businessmen and early volunteers had, however, left the railway in a much better state than when they found it. Ten years after the Society took the helm, traffic had increased from 5,235 passenger journeys (*i.e.* a one way trip) in 1950, *Sir Haydn*'s last season, to 67,018 by 1960 and the 185,574 that became the all time peak in 1973 which has never yet been equalled despite the extension over the mineral line to Nant Gwernol. The millionth passenger had been carried on 7th September 1971.

Recreating the beginning twenty-one years on. TR and local dignatories push the original train round No. 2 *Dolgoch* at Rhydyronen on the TRPS' 21st birthday on 15th May, 1972: James Boyd and his wife, local Councillors and Kay Adams (wife of the President John Adams) are amongst those providing the labour.

Abergynolwyn new station under a surprise fall of snow immediately after Easter in 1970. The building was then nearly a year old, having been opened on 28th May 1969 by Miss Stella Mair Owen, the National Hostess for Wales. The cast iron pillars supporting the canopy roof were rescued from BR's Towyn station. This building replaced a rather nondescript slate building with no facilities (somewhat similar to the original one still remaining at Brynglas) and has enabled the railway to offer catering and even weddings.

No. 4 *Edward Thomas* shunting the refreshment van onto the siding at Abergynolwyn, having brought it up at the head of the first train of the day circa 1966-67.

Whilst democracy now prevailed, the preservationists faced significant challenges. To cater for the huge increase in traffic, a new range of bogie carriages had been introduced, more passing loops created to enable three train sets to run simultaneously and new station buildings were planned and built at both Tywyn and Abergynolwyn. A further 'new' locomotive was sourced from the Irish Turf Board which, when rebuilt and adapted to the TR's requirements, would be the most powerful locomotive yet. In 1976, passenger services were extended from Abergynolwyn up the mineral extension to Nant Gwernol at the foot of the inclines to the quarries. Everyone thought, somewhat naturally, that passenger numbers would continue to increase as indeed they had done almost every year for the first twenty-one years of the TRPS' existence. But they did not. Traffic figures began to fall.

The way people were taking holidays in Britain was changing drastically. With very few exceptions, those who took holidays abroad before the Second World War were looking for adventure or to better their minds, not to lie around on beaches. Even in the immediate post-war period, travelling by road or rail across war-torn Europe was not easy. Horizon Holidays, probably the inventor of the package holiday, inaugurated summer flights from London to Corsica in a Douglas DC-3 aircraft, which made the journey at a top speed of 170mph in a mere six hours, including a refuelling stop at Lyon. Change had begun. In the 1960s

hotel construction developed rapidly in the Mediterranean and larger and faster aircraft became available, bringing economies of scale and reducing journey times to Mallorca to four and then three hours and, with the arrival of the first jets, to two hours. Gradually, restrictions on taking currency abroad were eased and when restrictions on package holiday pricing ceased in the 1980s, the demand for cheap holidays abroad was unstoppable. So the caravans in the farms under the mountains and by the sea reduced in number, as did the holidaymakers to the area. Most people now had cars and so were able to drive wherever and almost whenever they wanted to different places. As the economy improved in the 1970s and '80s, people demanded more choice, better quality and adventures. The advent of jet travel in aviation made faraway places increasingly accessible and the Boeing Jumbo 747 was a game changer, bringing in vast economies of scale which made holidays affordable almost anywhere in the world. People demanded experiences but the Talyllyn Railway offered only a charming slow and antiquated ride to nowhere in particular. It still attracted business though but only just enough passengers and, interestingly, only about the same number who patronised the line in the early 1950s. The revenue was not going to pay all the bills. But then, the preservationists in the early days never expected to and have continued happily to subsidise the line where necessary.

Times continue to change. Foreign travel was hit hard

No. 1 *Talyllyn* poses at Pendre. No. 1 was the first locomotive delivered to the railway, originally without its trailing axle which was added to provide better stability. By the Second World War, the locomotive was totally worn out and even the preservationists put *Talyllyn* out to grass under a barn to make way for the 'new' locomotives. However, Eric Gibbons offered to rebuild the locomotive at his Black Country workshops free of charge, an offer gladly accepted and No. 1 returned to service in 1957. Unfortunately, whilst the new component parts were well made, their assembly left a lot to be desired. Until the locomotive was rebuilt again under the supervison of John Bate, it continued to give trouble, although looked very attractive with its brass dome and chimney ring. Happily, following this subsequent rebuilding, *Talyllyn* is now once again a useful member of the locomotive fleet. [KC]

No. 2 *Dolgoch* poses at Pendre on 14th September 1963. No.2 is an interesting design, marketed as *'Fletcher Jennings' patent locomotive'* due to its long wheelbase and rear main axle positioned behind the firebox. This locomotive was the only one capable of use towards the end of Sir Haydn's lifetime and, reluctant though he was to spend money on the railway, he was obliged to send for repairs to the Atlas Works in Shrewsbury in the 1940s. Nicknamed the 'Old Lady', No. 2 gallantly persevered into the preservation years until the two Corris locomotives could shoulder all the work. Fascinatingly, it was only by sheer good luck that this was possible at all. When the boiler inspector came to check *Dolgoch* over at the beginning of the TRPS years, probably his first visit for many a year, he drilled a hole in possibly one of the few boiler plates still remaining thick enough to pass the test. Had he drilled a hole a few inches to the left or right, it might well have been game over for No. 2 which would, at the very least, have dealt a severe blow to the Society. After protracted delay due to worries over financing the new boiler, Eric Gibbons once again offered to rebuild No. 2 and she is now a reliable performer once again. [KC]

No. 5 *Midlander* poses at Pendre in original condition, apart from regauging from 2ft 6ins, on 27th July 1961. A standard Ruston four-wheeled diesel locomotive, she is so named as the Midland Area of the TRPS arranged and financed its purchase from a Northamptonshire quarry. [KC]

Instances of the haulage rope breaking on the two inclines up to the quarries was a hazard of the job. Most probably as a consequence of one such break, these slate wagons had run away down the Cantybredd Incline to rest in pieces and still abandoned in the Gwernol River in April 1968.

Cantrybedd Incline winding house in the last stages of decline, with only its walls just extant in April 1968. As a child, your author used to eye the leaning tower of slate with considerable trepidation as he walked through the remains, especially having been told they were unsafe.

The Road to Adventure. The mineral extension in original condition. When taking the annual summer train ride, the Whitehouse family used to walk up the track at least to the winding house but preferably all the way to Nant Gwernol (and even all the way into the quarries). Mrs Thelma Whitehouse can be seen walking along the track in April 1968. When the decision was taken to extend passenger services up this extension, no land title deeds to it could be found. It transpired that the Talyllyn Railway Company ended at the gate east of Abergynolwyn station and when Sir Haydn Jones purchased the railway company from the McConnel family, he bought the mineral extension personally. In preservation times, considerable tactful discussions took place to enable the company to take ownership of this part of the railway but, eventually, success was achieved, a Light Railway Order obtained and reconstruction begun.

'The Winding House has gone. It should have been kept, the ingenuity and effort required to keep it a challenge to our engineers, to provide one of the visual pleasures of the journey, and, for those who can look further, evocative evidence of the old crucial links between village, railway and mountain.' (Sonia Rolt). Seen in April 1968, the original winding house on the mineral extension at the top of the incline to the village was possibly a unique way of delivering goods required to a slate mining village. Sadly, this winding house was squarely in the path of the Nant Gwernol extension (indeed, the track ran right through the middle of the building) and it was also unsafe and so was demolished to allow the extension to be converted to passenger use. Some of its slate slabs were recovered and used in the construction of the new station at Abergynolwyn.

Success to the new railway. On the opening day of the mineral extension to passengers on 22nd May 1976, No. 2 *Dolgoch*, driven by Dai Jones and fired by Phil Guest, heads its second train to Nant Gwernol, past Pendre station specially decorated for the occasion.

by the Gulf War of 1990-91 and Saddam Hussein's threat to shoot down Western civilian aircraft. The 9/11 terror attacks caused global panic. It may be with global warming both bringing hotter summers to Britain and millennials encouraging governments to reduce and eliminate carbon emissions, that people will once again turn their attention to the Welsh coast for holidays, reachable by the electric car or hydrogen train to bask on sandy beaches in a sunny and hot climate. The recent increase in adventure seeking with zip wires, toboggan runs and go-karting in former slate quarries in North Wales may well be a pointer to charming narrow gauge railways like the Talyllyn to encourage them to offer experiences different to

just a seat on a train up the Fathew Valley. Already the TR's offer to drive your own steam train adds value and provides a talking point.

However, some things have never changed, and nor will they: the lasting effects of a good holiday, the anticipation of a trip to come, the joy of spending time with friends and the lasting memories these things all create. Like every other tourist attraction, the Talyllyn Railway just needs to ensure it is in the forefront of providing those memories, now and in the future, just as it did so well in times when perhaps holidaymakers were less demanding. The Talyllyn will do well to keep its charm and character and continue to run its original train from 1865.

Dreams do come true. Sonia Rolt described the extension project thus: *'For years the idea of Nant Gwernol has hovered, grail-like. A symbol of an eventual goal where everything the railway stood for could be expressed. There we shall be near the heart of the matter, Bryn Eglwys and the collapsing mountain chambers whose riches were the reason for our living presence today. Most beautiful, secret and moving in itself, the gorge and platform above the piercingly sweet clarity of the rushing waters below, are the place for us to make something new which does incorporate all we feel we should show to honour the past.'* **So, at Abergynolwyn station on 22nd May 1976, Chairman James Boyd makes a speech at the inauguration of the Nant Gwernol Extension, listened to by Pat Garland (with pipe), two of the inaugural team who began the journey to create the world's first voluntary run railway. Wynford Vaughan Thomas drove a gold plated spike into the sleepers to signify completion of the work. No. 2** *Dolgoch*, **took the invited guests up the new line to the strains of the band playing the time honoured railway opening tune of** *'See the Conquering Hero Comes'*.

The original train heads up the cutting from Towyn Wharf to Pendre just as it has done for over 150 years. No. 2 *Dolgoch* hauls the 21st anniversary train for the Talyllyn Railway Preservation Society on 15th May 1976.

Linda being loaded at Port Penrhyn on Friday 13th July 1962, for delivery by rail to the FR at Minffordd exchange sidings. Surprisingly, the BR crane crew had some difficulty getting *Linda* onto the Lowmac wagon. At this point in the proceedings, there was an animated discussion about what to do next because the crane had run out of lift and *Linda's* rear buffer beam was too low to clear the sloped end of the wagon. The person sitting on the sleepers taking a light reading is Don Hayter, the professional painter who painted many of the FR carriages in the 1950s and '60s. [John Dobson]

2
LINDA

Linda in Boston Lodge Bottom Yard on Sunday 15 July 1962. The upper part of the rear cab sheet was removed as soon as the locomotive arrived. Volunteers cleaned her up as far as was possible whilst steam was raised for her first test train, including Mike Davis, one of the 'Sheffield lads', who is still a current volunteer on carriage electrics and, to his immediate right, Bill Hoole (wearing grease top hat), formerly a driver on the East Coast Main Line. [John Dobson]

In the Autumn 1962 edition of the *Festiniog Railway Magazine*, the official voice of the railway, it was admitted that '*the main, but by no means the only, headache has been the locomotive situation*'. Although there were then two double engines in traffic, having both working simultaneously was a rarity as parts came loose and boilers leaked. In fact, in July, *Merddin Emrys*' firebox became a great cause for concern, leaking badly from the crown stays, resulting in a huge effort to keep any water at all in the locomotive's boiler. The railway was obliged to withdraw this double engine only four days before the summer peak season time table was due to start. The second double engine, *Earl of Merioneth*, only intended to be the spare locomotive, was pressed into service but the staff at Boston Lodge have a long history of enduring working days and maintenance nights!

The only other working locomotive was *Prince*. Whilst a surefooted small engine and part of a pack of six similar machines managing the peaks of the slate traffic in the 1880s with some panache, as an 0-4-0 tender tank engine designed in the 1860s it was hardly suitable to haul heavy loads of passengers in bogie carriages day in day out for months. *Prince* needed some assistance and urgently. Quite apart from being a small locomotive, *Prince* was not 100 per cent well either. He had managed to make a trip from Boston Lodge across the Cob embankment to Portmadoc without his regulator even being opened! He also had trouble with his valves and a broken piston head, which obviously did not help.

Fortuitously, the Penrhyn Quarry Railway nearby was planned to close and still had two working steam locomotives of more or less the same gauge. We will return to their gauge soon enough. Normally, they only used one locomotive at a time and, when approached, were happy enough to lend the other to the Festiniog Railway. *Linda* was hired for the summer season, being loaded onto a standard gauge wagon on Friday 13th July 1962, unloaded in Minffordd exchange yard onto the FR the following evening, reaching Boston Lodge on the Sunday morning. As needs must, she was steamed and that very evening took a trial train of six carriages to see how things went. The train got as far as Cei Mawr, the high embankment just north of the passing

Linda in Boston Lodge Bottom Yard soon after delivery on Sunday 15th July 1962, with two very proud (if rather grubby!) volunteer cleaners in attendance. [John Dobson]

Linda, still in Penrhyn black livery and paired with FR tender No. 38, climbs Creua bank shortly after leaving Minffordd.

loop now installed at Rhiw Goch, when the locomotive crew decided to retreat in case the coal and water supplies ran out. Nevertheless, it appeared that *Linda* had all the possibilities to solve the summer locomotive crisis, pairing with *Prince*. *Linda* was steamed almost daily, double-heading with *Prince* on the 2.15 and, on occasions, hauling trains on her own.

Bob Harris, sometime deputy Works Manager at Boston Lodge, had arrived on the railway as a fitter about the same time as *Linda*. He takes up the story of the engine joining the working fleet:

'When she was tried out for the first time, her valve timing was clearly out. Garraway, the General Manager, had her valves taken out for examination and, eventually, called Stevenson, the Penrhyn engineer, over together with one of the old drivers, Dick Roberts, to show how she used to be worked. Dick simply put her into full forward gear and drove off and everything sounded alright, so Garraway took over and gradually notched her back (main line practice) and the valve timing difference appeared straight away. Dick simply moved the reverser back to full forward (narrow gauge practice, quite unrefined). Garraway had some upgrading to do on Linda *now, but actually more than he thought. For no one knew then that she was the wrong gauge. All we had to go on was what James Boyd and Charles E. Lee had written about these railways and they simply referred to the Welsh lines as being two foot gauge and the Penrhyn 'main line' was thought to be the same as the FR; how wrong we were. However,* Linda *went through the point frogs alright and, as all the check rails along the line were worn, she seemed to manage fine, that is until she double-headed up the FR with* Prince. *This was necessary as* Prince *was obviously not working at full power and also as* Linda *was not then fitted with a vacuum brake, but simply had a vacuum hose with a brake valve fitted temporarily to the back of the cab. On one of these trips, on 5th*

September, Linda *objected to the FR track and simply leapt off it, only held from tipping over an embankment in the woods above Plas by* Prince*'s coupling connection. It was only then we found out that* Linda *was 1ft 10³/₄ins gauge whilst the FR was 1ft 11⁵/₈ins. The derailment was hushed up and pictures of it were banned.*

Over the winter of 1962-63, Linda's *wheels were sent to Hunslets and fitted with step tyres giving her an extra ³/₄in. width to bring her out to FR gauge. She was also provided with a tender, an old coal wagon, No. 38, formerly used as tender No .6 for 'Large England'* Little Giant, *with oil drums put inside to carry water. Later,* Welsh Pony's *tender was widened by 10ins and used instead, with No. 38 cascaded to* Blanche *which also came from Penrhyn at the end of 1963. Both locomotives were converted to left hand drive and fitted with vacuum brake equipment.*

Linda *was superheated in 1968 when her boiler was sent to Hunslets, who were also contracted to make two new double engine boilers. Allan Garraway adopted* Linda *as 'the ultimate engine' and so what could be better for new double engine boilers than two elongated* Linda *boilers placed back to back and welded together!'*

Around this time, the railway's insurers were getting twitchy about the steam locomotives setting fire to the woodland section of the railway and something had to be done. So, on 2nd November 1970, *Linda* emerged from Boston Lodge equipped with Laidlaw Drew oil-burning equipment, taking an empty five car set to Tan y Bwlch and back. At first, it was impossible to equal the performance of coal firing but, by modifying the burner to pass more oil and produce a near horizontal spray pattern and increasing the number of air tubes, *Linda* soon performed as well as ever, leading to the conversion of the rest of the locomotive fleet. One side effect of the oil firing conversion proved an

For the early test trains to Tan y Bwlch, *Linda* ran without a tender. On this occasion the test train was run in the evening, crossing the service train at Tan y Bwlch. The person in overalls at the extreme left is Tom Davies, the 'old company' driver who came back to drive in the 1950s and 1960s, having driven the last slate train on 1st August 1946; he was driving *Prince* on the evening service train. The guard of the evening train who is checking tickets may be William Wike. [John Dobson]

One of the first duties carried out by *Linda* after she had arrived on the FR was to collect a train of coal wagons from Minffordd. Driver Keith Catchpole attends to the fire whilst his fireman, Ned Quirk, takes a photograph. [John Dobson]

Linda was pressed into service immediately after arrival in July 1962, often double-heading with *Prince*. On one of these trips, on 5th September, *Linda* objected to the FR track and simply leapt off it, only held from tipping over an embankment in the woods above Plas by *Prince*'s coupling connection. The recovery and re-railing of *Linda* was a long and laborious process, achieved using screw jacks and sleeper cribs. The operation took around fourteen hours, extending into the small hours of the following day, but the railway was open for the first service train to run on time later that morning. Allan Garraway banned publication of all photographs and it is only relatively recently that the few which were taken have been published. The cause of the incident was *Linda* then being 1ft 10³/₄ins gauge and not the FR's gauge of 1ft 11⁵/₈ins. [John Dobson]

inability to keep the black paint on the smokebox due to the increased heat generated. Temporarily, the smokeboxes were painted aluminium, being the only heat resistant paint which could at first be found.

Linda proved to be of great value and, fortunately for the FR, the railway was able to negotiate not only her purchase but also that of her twin, *Blanche*, which arrived by road on 17th December 1963.

Very probably, these two locomotives were the best purchase the FR has ever made. Sixty-nine years old when they arrived, they both proved themselves sure footed, useful and popular motive power for all but the heaviest trains. By the time they reached their centenary, they had been responsible for more than one third of the locomotive mileage recorded since the beginning of the revival years. Built for the 'main line' of the Penrhyn Railway at Bethesda, they hauled slate down the private railway to the sea at Port Penrhyn, together with a third similar locomotive,

Charles, now splendidly restored in the National Trust's Penrhyn Castle Museum. Named after members of the quarrying owning family – Charles Douglas Pennant, his wife, Blanche, and their daughter, Linda – they had a near monopoly of all the slate traffic from their arrival in 1893, until *Blanche* hauled the last steam-worked train on 28th June 1962. Hunslet built very many 0-4-0STs for the slate industry but this trio were larger than most and their design slightly different, with cylinders inclined at 1 in 6 and with the coupling rods, unusually, placed inside the connecting rods giving them a quite distinctive appearance. This design enabled the cylinders to be brought closer together to reduce the width of the locomotive. Although, all locomotives were fitted with sandboxes, ahead of the water tank, the usual practice was to carry a bucket of sand perched on the front buffer beam, the fireman sanding by hand as necessary. On the Penrhyn Railway, all three locomotives were elegantly painted in black, lined out in red and blue.

Linda in original Penrhyn Railway condition but coupled with 'coal wagon No. 38' (previously *Little Giant*'s tender) approaches Boston Lodge in 1963 with an FR six-car set comprising original carriages and the former Lynton & Barnstaple carriage as a sign of things to come.

Linda in the same condition as the previous photograph, passing Boston Lodge with an Up train in 1963.

Linda at Porthmadoc in April 1972, sporting a silver smokebox and chimney after being converted to oil firing. Initially, suitable black paint could not be sourced which would adhere to the smokebox in the higher temperatures resulting from the use of this fuel.

Earl of Merioneth takes water at Porthmadoc in April 1969

3
BUILDING BACK TO BLAENAU

Boston Lodge works in almost original condition apart from one demolished stone tower gatepost on 27th August 1961. A young couple are happily walking down the track within a limited clearance area. Inside the works yard *Merddin Emrys* is standing on the inspection pit track having recently been returned to service, still with its old company wagon-top boiler but with new copper-capped tapered chimneys. [KC]

Samuel Holland, one of the pioneers of the North Wales slate industry, was born in 1803. When only eighteen years old, his father sent him to look after a new quarry which had opened at Rhiwbryfdir, in the parish of Ffestiniog. Holland had the quarry roads improved to carry slates to the river wharf, where they were taken by barge to the sea at Portmadoc. From there, schooners took the slates all over the world. One day, whilst at the Pen y Groes Inn, Holland met an Irishman, a Mr Henry Archer, and fell into conversation. Archer was thinking of renting the little horse railway between the quarries by Talysarn and Carnarvon. Holland advised him that '*if he really wished to undertake a railway, he had better come over to my neighbourhood and plan a railway from the Festiniog Quarries to Port Madoc.*' They walked over a possible route together. Archer was of the view that the railway should be a single line of only 2ft gauge so as to contain the cost of land and construction. They arranged for a Mr James Spooner to

be the engineer, formed a company by Act of Parliament and had a grand opening on 20th April 1836. The slate quarries were so successful and the railway became so busy that horse power could not do all the necessary work and it was decided to use steam power. George England of Hatcham in London built the steam locomotives, the first in the world on so small a gauge. James Spooner and his son, Charles, later fell in with a locomotive engineer named Robert Fairlie, who offered the railway a unique 'double engine' able to haul even more slates than the England-built ones. The first such engine proved his point. Named *Little Wonder*, it astounded the railway world by hauling double the previous tonnage with relative ease. In 1870, the Spooners sought to generate consultancy business for themselves and threw a party to demonstrate the prowess of the 'double engine' against the ordinary engine. Many foreigners came to witness the spectacle, including representatives from the court of the Tsar of Russia. The Festiniog Railway Company became

The rich heritage of the Ffestiniog Railway. Boston Lodge viewed from the hill top as one of the original 1863 locomotives, *Prince*, passes with a Down train bound for Portmadoc. In the yard, double engine *Merddin Emrys* and the First World War tractor *Moelwyn* can be seen together with the tanks from the second double engine, *Earl of Merioneth*. In Glan y Mor yard, in the foreground, both 'large England' *Welsh Pony* and the Harrogate Peckett 0-6-0ST are sheeted up on the right hand side and, on the left, FR bogie brake van No. 10, all awaiting restoration. The carpenters' shop is being extended to create a carriage works (now a locomotive shed) and one of the original bogie carriages is being rebuilt in the open air. A wide selection of waggons (the FR always referred to its own waggons spelt thus) can be seen in the view, ranging from the ubiquitous FR 2-ton slate waggons, FR wooden coal waggons to First World War bogie waggons full of coal.

Merddin Emrys hauls a train of carriages painted in 'Garraway green & ivory livery' over Cei Mawr, the highest stone embankment on the FR, just north of Rhiw Goch and before entering the SSSI woodland section running up to Tan y Bwlch. The first two vehicles behind the double engine are No. 8, the last remaining quarrymen's coach, and No. 2, an original brake van, both crammed full of happy enthusiasts.

famous all over the world as the template for narrow gauge railway systems.

Of course, success bred competition. Both the London & North Western and Great Western railways wanted a slice of the action and built competing lines to Ffestiniog. But, before the end of the 19th century, the slate market had peaked. Save for some spikes in demand due to world war damage, tiles took the lion's share of the roofing market. So, by the 20th century, the famous Festiniog Railway was largely in decline, but staggered on until the end of the Second World War and then expired. Many people wanted to reopen it as a tourist attraction, especially following the success of the Talyllyn Railway, a few miles down the coast, which was saved from oblivion by becoming the world's first volunteer run railway. By 1954, a scheme was worked out to acquire enough shares in the Festiniog Railway Company to take control and enthusiasts began to rehabilitate the famous line, working their way steadily up from the coast at Portmadoc, station by station. Allan Garraway was appointed manager and led the team on the ground both to operate the line and to extend it back up to the half way station, Tan y Bwlch. Trains reached there in 1958 and Garraway insisted that the line should not be reopened further until the operating section had all been put in good condition, capable of taking the increasing number of tourists who now clamoured for a ride

in the quaint train running through scenic Snowdonia. He was right to insist on a pause but the Festiniog *cognoscenti* were still restless: they wanted 'their' railway to return to Blaenau, whose slate quarries caused the line to be built in the first place and they would not rest until they succeeded.

'Back to Blaenau' has always been part of the Ffestiniog Railway mystique; ever since the reopening in 1955, its passenger time table included stations at Tanygrisiau and Blaenau Ffestiniog at the northern end of the line but with the note '*service temporarily suspended*'.

Garraway was of the view that the line to Tan y Bwlch was about the right length for a tourist railway and extending it further, whilst that might be nice, would simply require more capital which the railway did not have, increase operating costs and require ticket prices to be too high for a journey which was longer than most families sought: it would be a two hour return run. The editor of the in-house magazine, a wry wit named Dan Wilson sympathised: '*Superficially it cannot be said that Blaenau shapes up well for the job. Its thrice Portmadoc's rainfall, menacing slate tips and sheep eating out of dustbins gives it an aura which mesmerises.*'

But the Festiniog enthusiasts would not give up, despite the formidable obstacles that lay in their path, and there were many. They dreamed, discussed, planned, plotted and put their shoulders to the wheel. And, in 1982, the first train of

Double Fairlie *Merddin Emrys* stands at Portmadoc with a Down train at Easter 1972. The double engine sports driver Evan Davies' 'white wall tyres', which were all the rage on sports cars at the time. The power bogies and boiler frame are the only key remaining parts of the locomotive following renewal of the boiler and new welded side tanks but it is still working as a coal burner.

Earl of Merioneth, the second and last double engine built at Boston Lodge by the 'old company' in her last season of use, seen here on 10th April 1971 standing in front of the Britannia Foundry at Portmadoc, soon to be a memory itself. This locomotive has undergone no less than four name changes to date. Originally named *Livingston Thompson* after an early Chairman of the FRC, its name was changed to *Taliesin* to perpetuate the name carried by the much loved single Fairlie when that was scrapped. In the revival years, its name was changed again to *Earl of Merioneth*, one of the titles held by the Duke of Edinburgh, reputedly in an attempt to interest him in the line but without success. Now the locomotive has been withdrawn from service, it has reverted to its original name, *Livingston Thompson*. 'The Old Earl', as the locomotive is still affectionately known, after its name was transferred to a new build, remains in original style, preserved on static display at the National Railway Museum, following an outcry when the FRC proposed to dismantle it and use parts in a new build. Following much lobbying by an 'Active Forty' of horrified volunteers, the basic superstructure of the locomotive was retained.

Prince, one of the original four locomotives built by George England at Hatcham in London and delivered as long ago as 1863 (but rebuilt many times since then), stands on Boston Lodge curve on 1st April 1964, refitted with a straight frame and returned to service by the revival regime in 1955. This type of locomotive was the mainstay of the railway in its heyday of high slate traffic after taking over from horses. Four out of the eventual six similar locomotives have survived to the present day. *Prince* is painted in the green livery adopted after 1955, although a similar livery was in use during the inter war years. [KC]

ABOVE: The original wooden station building at Tan y Bwlch seen on 10th June, 1965 [KC]

BELOW: Pen Cob Halt on 27th August 1961, at the south end of the Cob next to the entrance to Boston Lodge Halt, with Moel y Guest towering above Portmadoc at the north end. [KC]

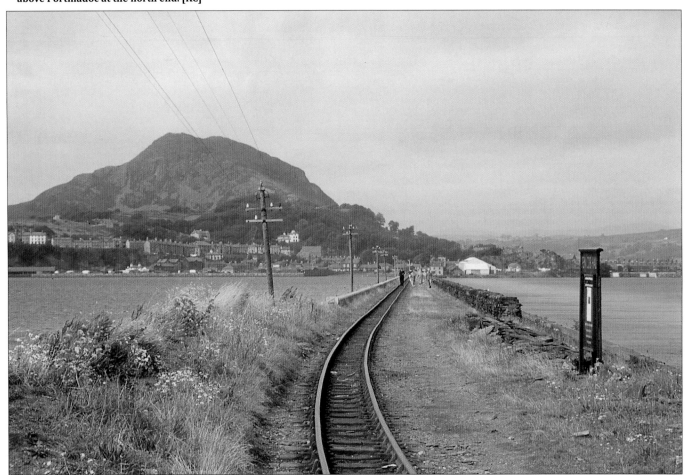

Moelwyn at Dduallt on the shuttle service between there and Tan y Bwlch, formed of No. 2 van, 'bug boxes' No's 3 and 4, and No. 8 quarrymen's van.

Blanche, repainted in full FR lined green livery and with her new tender cab but still as an 0-4-0, stands resplendent on Boston Lodge curve on 10th April 1966. [KC]

the revival years steamed proudly into Blaenau Ffestiniog. The railway's publicity suggested that this remarkable achievement would mark the beginning of a new era for the railway and could well double its potential as a tourist attraction of the decade to come. It was recalled that over half of the tourist passenger journeys between the wars originated at Blaenau, so all was expected to augur well. In fact, Garraway was proved right; traffic numbers fell but costs went up. The Festiniog Railway had given its all to get to Blaenau and was going to have to do more than that to boost traffic. Fortunately, Festiniog Railway people never give up.

The hurdles to climb to get to Blaenau were immense. Following abandonment in 1946, the whole railway became moribund, covered in brambles, bushes and, in parts, even trees. Re-opening, initially achieved in 1955, required everything to be repaired and the ancient steam locomotives coaxed back into action. Fortunately, one of the original 1863 steam locomotives, *Prince*, had been stored in the workshops with a new boiler ordered but not fitted before the railway closed. So *Prince* was soon back in action together with some of the original carriages. In addition, two double engines also survived and great efforts were made to get them both back into service whilst the line was cleared, station by station, from Portmadoc, along the Cob embankment to Boston Lodge, through the villages of Minffordd and Penrhyndeudraeth and then into the hills and ancient woodlands to the halfway station at Tan y Bwlch, where the wife of one of the platelayers, Bessie Jones,

dressed in traditional Welsh costume, met the trains and sold passengers postcards and ice creams.

The railway quickly proved popular in the growing tourist market and traffic outgrew capacity in the early revival years from 1955 to 1968, whilst trains ran no further than halfway. By 1965, the railway recorded 137,000 passenger journeys, by 1967, 200,000 and, by 1971, after the extension to Dduallt opened, 366,457. The locomotives were running around 7,000 miles each year to cope. More locomotives and more carriages were needed, together with improved track. Fortunately, the nearby Penrhyn slate quarry closed its own railway in 1962 and this allowed the acquisition of two of its steam locomotives of nearly the same gauge which were altered to become '*disgustingly reliable*'. New carriages were built and old ones repaired. Buffet and observation cars were created with corridor connections allowing catering and souvenir sales throughout the trains. All of the new carriages were produced in the company's well equipped Boston Lodge workshops.

Despite a decade of consolidation from 1958 onwards, an eye was had to extending the line above Tan y Bwlch back to the holy grail of Blaenau Ffestinog. Gradually, the next three miles of line were reconditioned, through the 'short' Garnedd tunnel, up to a halt in the middle of absolutely nowhere called Dduallt in time for passenger trains to run there again for Easter 1968. However, continuing from there proved much more troublesome. The Central Electricity Generating Board had obtained the North Wales Hydro-Electricity Act

Linda, repainted in full FR lined green livery, paired with withdrawn England *Welsh Pony's* tender, widened somewhat but not yet with a leading pony truck fitted, poses on Boston Lodge curve on 2nd April 1964. [KC]

Merddin Emrys, one of two double engines built at Boston Lodge by the 'old company' using Robert Fairlie's Patent design, poses on Boston Lodge curve on 27th August 1961 following return to service, still with its wagon top boiler but with new welded water tanks and new tapered copper-capped chimneys. [KC]

No. K1, the first ever Garratt articulated type of locomotive, built by Beyer, Peacock & Co. in 1909 for use in Tasmania, seen here on display outside Portmadoc Harbour station on 10th April 1966. When her service days finished, her manufacturers brought her back (amalgamated with some parts from her sister, No. K2) to display at their Gorton works in Manchester. When Beyer, Peacock closed, the FR purchased her really just to ensure she was preserved as a unique artefact but also with an eye to modification to help with the increasing traffic, although this would have required major surgery to ensure she fitted within the FR's very restricting loading gauge. Dan Wilson, editor of the *Festiniog Railway Magazine* summed up the emotional purchase like this: *'She was the sort of locomotive that we imagined running on the Festiniog only in our more lyrical dreams. The Garratt is not, of course, 'train ready.' She is too high, needs firebox attention and there is a suspicion that her low pressure cylinders will fit some of our narrower clearances like wheat in a sack; but she is the Little Wonder of her type and posterity would judge her as a unique and wholly appropriate acquisition.'* When the FR converted to oil firing, such butchery to No. K1 was considered really quite seriously and your author well remembers spending a day with the then Works Manager, Paul Dukes, greasing up the Garratt and protecting her from the elements whilst stored in Glan y Mor yard in the early 1970s. Paul gestured, with a wicked grin, that he looked forward to slicing bits off the superstructure to make it fit. Even then, your author silently determined that he would do what he could to ensure this never happened and, finally, had his wish come true when he arranged for the Garratt to be removed from display at the National Railway Museum and put back into service, in original style, on the rebuilt Welsh Highland Railway. [KC]

Palmerston, possibly the first narrow gauge steam locomotive to see service in the British Isles and one of four built for the start of locomotive-hauled services in 1863 by George England & Co., lies nearly derelict and literally put out to grass in Glan y Mor yard to await its fate on 8th July 1967. Then regarded as a 'no hope' project, *Palmerston* was eventually put up for sale by the FRC at £500. A correspondent wrote to the railway's in house magazine to say: *'Although I will concede that the locomotive has some sentimental value, it is little more than an eyesore and, if it is admitted that there is insufficient money available to restore* Princess *and* Welsh Pony *[sister locomotives], there can be no logical reason for* Palmerston's *retention.'* Fortunately, logic did not prevail and, although the locomotive was indeed sold, with a restrictive covenant that the new owners could not use her within 50 miles of the FR, emotion prevailed and *Palmerston* was rebuilt, returned to the FR and is now well loved and highly regarded. Before the locomotive left the railway, it had to suffer the indignity of being painted pink and renamed *Harold Wilson* as a joke for AGM day so as to become a founding member of the 'Dead Prime Minister' Class! [KC]

Earl of Merioneth running round its train at Dduallt using the original formation in April 1971. Note that the deviation spiral was under construction to the right.

allowing it to requisition the railway between Dduallt and Tanygrisiau, without paying any compensation, to enable a pumped storage electricity scheme to be constructed, which would flood the line above the 'long' Moelwyn Tunnel. If the Festiniog Railway was ever to get reconnected to Blaenau Ffestiniog it would have to build a new line round the obstacle of the new reservoir. So that is exactly what it set out to do.

The FR had a two-pronged strategy. First, it sued the CEGB to pay for reinstating the railway. Second, it devised a scheme of reconstruction to reconnect to the 'old' railway at Tanygrisiau. Both were bold. In respect of the litigation, the FR initially lost but it regrouped and sued instead for loss of profits, a battle which it won in 1971 after the longest fight in legal history. That resulted in £106,000 being paid to the FR. A lot of money but not enough to build a new section of line.

The civil engineering solution required the new railway to gain height to by-pass the new reservoir and then run alongside it to reconnect to the old Tanygrisiau station, three and a half miles away. This was achieved by means of the first spiral on any passenger carrying line in Britain. Such a device enabled the new line to gain the required height between two immoveable points (Dduallt station and the new reservoir) by creating more space to do so and, by incorporating a reasonable gradient, the steam trains could climb without difficulty. The spiral was as effective as it was unique: a vast sweeping curve, 3,500ft long, lifted the railway some 30ft higher. Construction began in 1965 by volunteers who quickly became known as the 'Deviationists' and the

line they were building 'The Deviation.' It was a phenomenal project, made even more so by the vast majority of it being delivered in the time honoured way of digging, using picks, shovels and wheelbarrows, with skips running on temporary track to shift something like 75,000 tons of material.

The Deviationists were a completely different set of people from those running the railway. Many came simply because of the engineering challenge in the Welsh hills. They shacked up in a wooden mess hut erected next to the south portal of the old Moelwyn Tunnel and gradually, yard by yard, created a new railway. A new Moelwyn Tunnel had to be built through the granite mountain and, for this, some Cornish mining engineers were contracted to help. In 1977, passenger trains ran up the spiral and through the new tunnel for the first time to a temporary terminus alongside the new reservoir, Llyn Ystradau. The deviation connected to Tanygrisiau in 1978 and then to Blaenau Ffestiniog, at a new station in the centre of town. On 25th May 1982, marking the 150th anniversary of the Royal Assent to the original Festiniog Railway Company Act of 1832, the official re-opening train triumphantly entered the station, hauled by double engine *Merddin Emrys*. The iron resolve of the Ffestiniog Railway Company had not wavered. The very considerable volunteer effort had restored and re-opened the whole Ffestiniog Railway. A quite remarkable achievement.

All this effort to fulfil the dream of 'Back to Blaenau' had cost a lot of money. True, some had come from the CEGB, plus grants and donations, together with considerable volunteer sweat. But much cash also had to be borrowed, which was to prove a millstone round the railway's neck for years. And the 'passenger explosion' had come to an end. Now the railway had an increased length of line which cost more to run and required more rolling stock to operate it. There was no cash to spare for anything but the bare minimum of requirements and it was to take years before the railway became debt free; about twenty years in fact. Allan Garraway had been proved right in his forecast that, in reality, the railway operating only to Tan y Bwlch was probably sustainable. But the FR is an ungrateful mistress and replaced Allan as General Manager for another who, in changing times, had the remit to make the railway more efficient, get it in better condition and make it more popular. To become so required superhuman effort but the team were largely up for that. The railway now had to withstand passenger traffic dwindling, redundancies and an entirely new way of working to survive and gradually build up its brand to enable it to change gear and enter the 20th century. This it did, and now it is one of the foremost tourist attractions in North Wales.

In April 1969, one of the new corridor carriages, quickly nicknamed 'Barns', receives finishing touches outside the extended former carpenters' shop and the new carriage works, supervised by John Halsall. The 'Barns' were new corridor carriages built to the same profile as the Lynton & Barnstaple No. 14 carriage rescued from that line's Snapper Halt. The 'Barn' nickname is an FR play on words, combining part of the 'Barnstaple' in the L&BR with the frequently found humour commenting on the capacious size of the new fleet!

Earl of Merioneth arrives at Portmadoc with a Down train, now all in red livery and including five 'Barns', passing *Blanche* standing at the station headshunt. Evan Davies, one of the double engine regular drivers, who had insisted on painting the wheel tyres white – all the rage in the 1960s – also had his own chime whistle, that he fitted on whichever engine he drove!

Merddin Emrys hauls an Up train nearing the short Garnedd Tunnel in high season on 21st August 1972.

Moelwyn with a train of original 1865 built 'Birminghams', nick named 'Bug boxes', at Portmadoc station in 1968, on the spur leading to the goods shed and the former Welsh Highland Railway connection. *Moelwyn* was a useful opportune purchase by Colonel Stephens when he ran the FR in the late 1920s and was intended to replace an England engine as a shunter in the slate yards. Named *Moelwyn* in the revival years, this was another FR humourist play on words reflecting Baldwin, the makers of the locomotive and the nearby mountains of the same name where 'Moel' means 'bald' in Welsh!

Deviation at Archer's Dam on 16th April 1974. A temporary bridge made of sleepers has been built where the dam has been breached to allow the new railway to pass through. In the foreground, a deviationist is gravitating down the grade on a skip wagon, interestingly in the very same year as the Health & Safety at Work Act was introduced! *'This is how it goes for the weekend, with halts at 2pm for bread and cheese, pickled onions, jam or honey and apples, bananas and chocolate.'*

New flat bottom track on Dduallt spiral.

Moelywn Tunnel south portal in April 1980, emphasising the very narrow bore. Woe betide any train which ran out of steam in the tunnel in the 'old company days'. The fireman would be obliged to squeeze out of the cab in the very limited clearance and uncouple the locomotive from the train, so it could draw clear out of the tunnel before asphyxiating the passengers with a tunnel full of smoke.

A Smalley digger at Moelwyn Tunnel north end on 16th April 1974. The Deviation launched a scheme to raise money to buy this useful machine by collecting innumerable Green Shield stamps, at that time given away to incentivise motorists to use participating garages to fill up their cars with petrol rather than their competitors. Fortunately, a well wisher got to hear of the Deviation and presented the railway with the Smalley, so allowing the Green Shield stamps to be cashed in for many other useful machine tools.

The new deviation spiral takes shape at Dduallt with temporary contractors' track laid towards the new Rhoslyn bridge over the original main line.

Garnedd Tunnel before restoration. Originally, before the tunnel existed, the horse-worked line ran round the hillside to the right and this formation can still be seen. There was an embryo scheme to dismantle the tunnel and return to this formation as there were some fears that its condition was deteriorating, coupled with the thoughts about running Garratts purchased for the new Welsh Highland Railway up the FR, which would not fit through the tunnel. Fortunately, light hearted threats of forming a 'Garnedd Tunnel Preservation Society' may have dissuaded the FRC board of these erroneous thoughts. [KC]

Moelwyn mess, a wooden sectional timber hut measuring 60ft by 20ft that was used as a dormitory and mess hut, with the twelve bed units later expanded to twenty-four. This was built on the old track formation at the far end of a stone embankment and in front of Moelwyn Tunnel south portal for use by the Deviationists. On 16th April 1974, the old railway formation is still in place running from Dduallt station right up to the hut, so providing a siding right up to the front door! A stream of water within the tunnel, which always had water seepage even when in use, provided the Deviationists with a ready supply of running water.

Awaiting restoration. Original FRC bullhead track lies partly buried in the grass on 11th April 1971, as the line wends its way past cottages at Tanygrisiau.

Newly laid track at the same location.

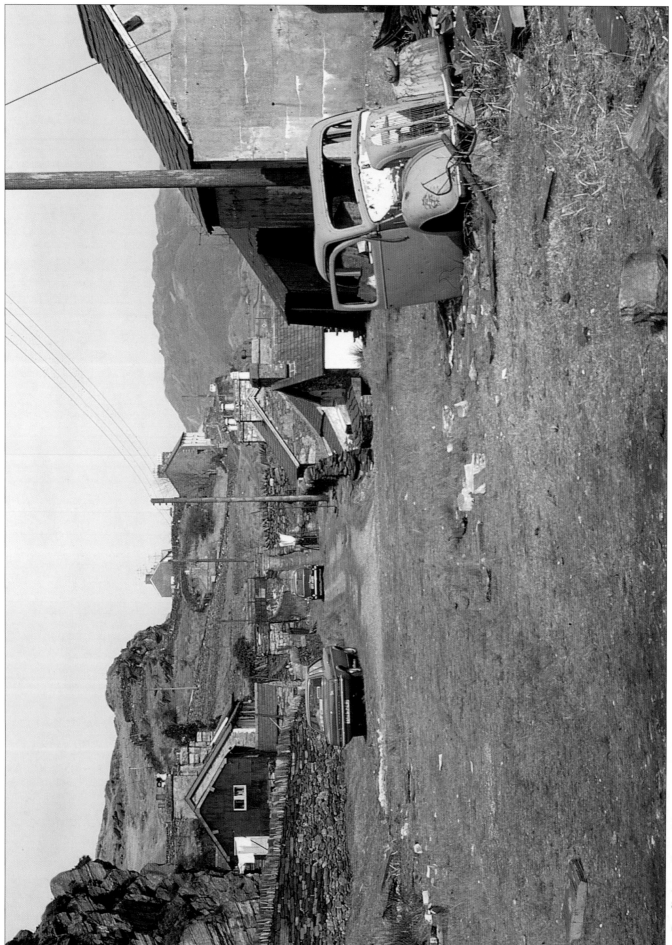

Dereliction at Tanygrisiau station. [KC]

Old FR locomotive shed at Glan y Pwll on 11th April 1971.

Princess was the last locomotive in service in the 'old company' days and has never been modified or changed from its then condition and is now kept as a 'museum piece' and used as a roving ambassador for the railway. She is seen here plinthed at Blaenau Ffestiniog between the old FR 'Stesion Fein' as a statement of intent to return services to the town.

Blanche takes water at Tan y Bwlch in April 1968.

The two Americans at Portmadoc in August 1972. Train locomotive *Mountaineer*, piloted for convenience by *Moelwyn* as far as Tan y Bwlch, where the diesel would the take up running Dduallt shuttle duties using the 'bug boxes' in between every service train. It had been found that folk were turning up at Tan y Bwlch expecting a ride on the main trains which were packed, sometimes with standing room only, so the shuttles were introduced to enable the railway to relieve what would otherwise be disappointed passengers of some much needed cash.

Mountaineer, complete with original FR bell from the long time scrapped England 0-4-0T of the same name, leaves Minffordd on Easter Monday, 30th March 1970. *Mountaineer* was built as a 2-6-2T by the American Locomotive Company in 1916 for the First World War and saw service at the French front, then continued in use at Pithiviers until rescued and donated to the FR. It is commonly referred to as 'the Alco', reflecting its builder, and proved to be a very indifferent steamer until converted to oil firing, which transformed its performance. However, with American, French and English nuts and bolts, it was to cause some headaches to the works staff.

A line of three FR carriages, headed by Ashbury built No. 22, all freshly painted in a new red livery, which was rather startling when straight out of the paint shop, all seen in the sidings at Portmadoc at Easter in 1969. Fortunately, the red colour toned down quite quickly after a short exposure to the elements but was soon altered to maroon with cream upper panels, which remains the carriage livery today.

No. 14, the ex-Lynton & Barnstaple carriage adapted to the FR loading gauge which became the pioneer of a new fleet of modern Festiniog Railway carriages, seen in the platform at Porthmadog on 13th April 1974 (the spelling changed from Portmadoc in 1974). Fred Boughey commented on car No. 14 as follows: *'Experience with No. 12 had shown that a buffet car was an extremely lucrative proposition. The rebuilding of the remains of the L&B coach into the impressive and serviceable vehicle it is today forms an important chapter in the recent history of FR's coaching stock, since the fundamental design for the new stock which was to follow was to a considerable extent evolved from it.'*

4
MAENOFFEREN AND THE LAST SLATE INCLINE IN NORTH WALES

The Back Vein Incline at Maenofferen in August 1972; three tracks descend into the mountain.

Maenofferen, Slate Quarry Co. Ltd was incorporated in 1861 and became one of the many Blaenau Ffestiniog quarries to ship slate over the Festiniog Railway. In 1908, it leased wharf space in the FR's exchange yard with the Cambrian Railways at Minffordd. Its slate shed there survives with the company name on the gable end. When the FR closed in 1946, Maenofferen leased a short length of track between Duffws station and the BR interchange in Blaenau until 1962 and continued to operate slate trains within the town, albeit hauled by diesels until road transport took over. Within the quarry complex, internal tramways, and balanced and electrically worked inclines still continued in use, more or less unchanged, until 1976. This was the particular attraction for Festiniog volunteers when they were not working on the railway. There was nowhere else an authentic slate quarry system could be seen – and played with – in the 1970s ... unofficially of course!

Several of the FR permanent staff were interested in the quarries too. Ron Lester, head of permanent way, used to take intrepid volunteers into the tunnels at Cwmorthin to see the underground inclines. Norman Gurley, also a pw employee, took us into the quarry systems at Dorothea and Pen yr Orsedd on summer evenings. Like many FR volunteers before us, we caught the bug and went exploring ourselves. Maenofferen beckoned after high tea.

We parked our car at the foot of No. 2 Incline (the No. 1 Incline down to Duffws station had been disused since 1962), walked up and along the Rhiwbach Tramway, with its grass grown uneven rails, marveling at the slate-built winding houses with their levers and cables, all then still in use. At the summit, we were in the quarry mill and stack yard where all the finished slate was neatly stacked in its various sizes by the large and long slate mill. Better still, on the rails in the yard were dozens of FR slate waggons used to ferry the finished slates from the mill, down the No. 2 Incline for loading into lorries. Of course, it was impossible not to try to move a slate waggon. Easy! So, we spent many happy evenings running slate waggons all over the yard, through

With the Moelwyn mountains as backdrop, we look down at the dereliction within Maenofferen slate quarry in August 1972. To the right, Incline No. 2 of the Rhiwbach Tramway can be seen still clinging on to life, with both loaded and empty FR slate waggons at its foot. This is as far as the railway system went in 1972, as a road way has been cut to the foot of the incline to collect the slate and also join the quarry to Llechwedd next door, so making Incline No. 1 (which took the tramway down to the FR station at Duffws) redundant. Now, the road has also been continued up to the top of the quarry making Incline No. 2 redundant as from 1976.

MAENOFFEREN AND THE LAST SLATE INCLINE IN NORTH WALES

the points and making trains up, using ourselves as motive power. We could not find one of the Ruston & Hornsby diesel locomotives on our visits but older volunteers bragged that they had and even started them up and did some proper shunting! We had a whale of a time. One evening, being particularly brave, we got a rake of slate waggons rolling really very well but were unable to stop them before they banged into some stationary ones. Whilst there were no derailments or any damage, the noise of the waggons hitting each other reverberated round the mountains with a huge echo. It was time to beat a hasty retreat to the pub.

But we had seen enough to whet our appetite to go underground and also see the inclines working. A little further on from the slate mill, past the weighbridge and through a small tunnel, we found the Back Vein Incline, three tracks which disappeared underground into a huge hole in the mountainside. Peering into the dirty windows of the winding house, which controlled the ropes on the incline, we could see three large well-oiled steel rope winding drums and levers. The very last slate quarry inclines still in use inside a mountain. We just had to see all this working.

Nothing ventured, nothing gained, through contacts in the FR permanent way department, we wrote to the quarry and asked. They replied and, as we were FR volunteers, they said yes. We were to have our own private tour of a working slate quarry! But only for an hour and during the lunch break period.

On the appointed day, we turned up at the office, signed the indemnity forms and straight away, we were led into the mountainside through one of the tunnels, walking along the railway tracks and alongside a channel of water being pumped out of the mountain. The tunnel led to one of the huge cathedral like chambers inside which miners climbed ladders to drill holes preparatory to controlled explosions to bring down the next blocks of slate for the cutting mill. We were in awe at the sheer size of the chamber deep inside the mountain, dimly lit by some electric lights. A Ruston & Hornsby diesel locomotive, fitted with an exhaust conditioner, was throbbing away pouring out fumes whilst coupled to some slab waggons destined for the Back Vein Incline. And so were we.

Our guide walked us to the foot of the triple track incline and gestured for us to climb aboard one of the wooden passenger carrying vehicles for a trip up the incline itself. This was better than our wildest dreams! With a shout and a wave to the winding house, the driver there rang the bell and machinery inside began to whir. Slowly, steadily and yawing slightly from side to side, we were hauled up to the top. Now we could look inside the winding house and stand on the driver's platform itself. There we came up close to

Another view of the three tracks of the Back Vein Incline at Maenofferen descending into the mountain in August 1972.

Loaded slate waggons wait at the end of their journey at the foot of No. 2 Incline in August 1972. The slates would be transferred to road transport when sufficient had accumulated.

[ABOVE] Inside the cutting shed in August 1972, showing the booths for the slate makers to sit and deftly cut slabs of slate into roofing material.

[BELOW] On the left can be seen the saw tables which cut crossways through the blocks of slate so they were then a size which could be handled by one man and split with a chisel into very thin wafers. On the right, the slate waste was loaded into waggons ready to be tipped to increase the mountains of rubbish slate dominating Blaenau Ffestiniog.

Three winding drums glistening with oil inside the winding house at the top of the Back Vein Incline in August 1972, having just hauled us up the incline out of the slate caverns inside the mountain.

the three winding drums and the gear which worked them – levers to engage the clutches driving the drums and the handbrake. This winding house, originally steam worked, was now electrically operated and the speed of its motors was managed by a simple but effective use of liquid controllers. By moving a lever, metal plates were lowered into barrels full of brine, which boiled alarmingly, but the speed of the motors increased the further the plates were lowered into the barrels. Even in the 1970s you would pinch yourself at seeing this sight working for real outside a museum but this method continued in use until the 1990s.

Walking back through the short tunnel, we entered the huge and long slate mill in the main yard and were able to see the whole process of preparing slates. First the huge blocks of slate were split along the grain, then hauled onto a saw table which cut through the block crossways so they were then a size which could be handled by one man and split with a chisel into very thin wafers. We even tried the art itself and experienced the marvel of the slate splitting cleanly and perfectly into two. Then the slates were trimmed to size on a dressing machine to produce the finished roofing slate, all kept in sizes in the mill stock yard until required. The waste was loaded into a rubbish waggon and pushed out onto one of the tips, all very visible landmarks in the region.

Underground production at Maenofferen

Inside the Maenofferen slate mill in July 1977. Bobby Jones, slate maker, was at work using the splitting chisel to reduce the large slabs on the right hand side of the picture into thin slates. The slabs were split into half thickness and then each part halved once again, so keeping an equal weight of slate on either side of the chisel. [Ann Hatherill]

Maenofferen mill yard, with cut slates stacked ready for loading together with original FR 2-ton slate waggons loaded for their journey down the Rhiwbach No. 2 incline in August 1972.

MAENOFFEREN AND THE LAST SLATE INCLINE IN NORTH WALES

ceased in November, 1999 and with it came the end of large scale underground working for slate in North Wales. The heyday of the quarry was in the 1890s, when 14,000 tons of finished slate were produced each year by 400 employees. Now, Maenofferen has been 'untopped' to enable high quality slate to be recovered from the pillars supporting the chambers at each level within the mountain. An understandable commercial development but with it comes significant destruction of a past world which provided a livelihood for very many Welshmen making much profit for the wealthy and powerful. Whilst still working on an open cast basis, the world has moved on and, indeed, the slate industry failed to adapt to changes in demand for roofs and has suffered a long drawn out decline. Little is left for a possible World Heritage status for slate quarries in Wales. How fabulous it would have been to be able to keep Maenofferen in its original state for future generations to learn from. We were very lucky to see it working 'for real.'

The Great Western Railway manufactured 2-ton slate waggons when it entered the market by driving a branch line to Blaenau Ffestiniog from Bala. As late as August 1972, some of these were still in service at Maenofferen slate quarry, easily identified by the company's initials.

Cut slates neatly stacked in sizes and marked in batches, in August 1972, ready to be lifted into former FR waggons for their journey down the Rhiwbach No. 2 incline and then by road to the customer.

In June 1976, a Ruston diesel locomotive propels six loaded slate waggons across the Barllwyd channel and under the bridge onto the Rhiwbach Tramway, heading for the No. 2 Incline. The No. 3 Incline (disused) is to the right. The bridge above the train carries the line to the slate tips, originally worked by the Bagnall steam locomotives. In the top left of the picture can be seen the roof of the Maenofferen slate mill, with the former steam locomotive shed seen through the bridge railings in the top centre of the picture. [Ann Hatherill]

The loaded slate waggons having arrived in the loop at the top of No. 2 Incline in June 1976, the men are preparing for them to be sent down it by first oiling the points. Idris Owen, the brakesman, is changing his spectacles before walking up to the brakesman's platform in front of the winding house drum, from where he will manage the safe descent of the waggons by controlling the speed the rope drum rotates. [Ann Hatherill]

In June 1976, two loaded slate waggons stand at the top of the No. 2 Incline, the position known as 'the crimp,' waiting for crewling to begin. The chain connecting them to the winding house rope is attached to the rear waggon coupling. The view shows the double track from the incline merging into a single track and then branching out again into a loop where empty waggons are waiting to be taken up to the quarry mill yard. Idris Owen, the incline brakesman, is standing on the brakesman's platform in front of the winding house. The men are waiting for the signal from the bottom of the incline that all is ready to begin the run. When this is received, the wheelstop in front of the leading waggon will be removed and the waggons eased over the edge of the crimp at the top of the incline, taking up the slack in the rope and commencing the run down by gravity, with Idris handling the brake. [Ann Hatherill]

A close-up of brakesman Idris Owen holding the brake lever connected to the winding house rope drum at the top of No. 2 Incline in June 1976. With this lever he could manually control the speed of slate waggons descending and ascending by gravity and bring them safely to a stand at the foot of the incline. [Ann Hatherill]

Originally, the loaded slate waggons continued their journey by rail down the No. 1 incline into Duffws station yard and from there by Festiniog Railway to the Maenofferen stock shed at Minffordd exchange yard. Even when the FR closed, the quarry leased a short section of the railway to run its own trains from the foot of the incline to the slate yard at Blaenau Ffestiniog but then, towards the end of rail operations at Maenofferen, slate was transferred to road at the foot of the No. 2 incline. Here in September 1978, the slates are being transferred into wooden crates onto an articulated lorry for further transportation. [Ann Hatherill]

In June, 1977, David and Mary Hatherill watch a short run of empty slate waggons ascending the No. 2 Incline from Maenofferen, the last working incline in the Blaenau Ffestiniog quarries. The descending loaded waggons can be seen at the top of the picture. [Ann Hatherill]

The view down the Rhiwbach No. 2 incline in August 1972. Both loaded and empty slate waggons can be seen in the sidings at the foot. The cable which will haul the next rake of empty slate waggons up to the quarry rests in between the rails on the left hand incline track.

5
AN EXPERIENCE
ABOVE EVERYTHING ELSE

Recently, the view from the summit of Snowdon was voted the best in the United Kingdom. The breathtaking view from the peak beat the likes of Stonehenge, Loch Ness, the Palace of Westminster and Giant's Causeway to be named the nation's favourite. The easiest way to see this view is to take a quaint rack-assisted train.

In 1894, a tourist railway up Snowdon, the highest mountain in Wales, became a reality with a company being formed to build and operate it as a rack-assisted railway. It is unique in Britain. The Swiss led the world in the application of technology to railways climbing mountains. So, the Snowdon Mountain Tramroad & Hotels Co. Ltd simply ordered Swiss equipment for their own railway: five steam locomotives built

by the Swiss Locomotive & Machine Co. of Winterthur and made to metric specification, together with the Abt system for the rack and pinion running rails to enable the locomotives to climb the mountain safely on grades up to 1 in 5. Apart from the well known shaky start when trains ran away on the opening day, the mountain railway settled down to a popular but fairly uneventful way of life as a commercial concern purely for holiday passengers. Its fortunes were subject only to the vagaries of the mountain weather and interruptions in tourist traffic by two world wars. It has always been popular as it offers a unique ride and experience up Wales' highest mountain, with the Summit station being at 3,493 feet above sea level and the railway climbing 3,140 feet.

It may be thought that climbing a mountain at so steep an

No. 2 *Enid* stands on Llanberis shed with an open wagon. *Enid* was built in 1895 (SLM Works No. 924) and is named after Assheton-Smith's daughter, who performed the cutting of the first sod ceremony for the building of the railway. The Assheton-Smiths owned the Snowdon mountain and the Dinorwic quarries and the land in between. No. 2 was reboilered at Port Dinorwic in 1922-23 and overhauled by Hunslets of Leeds in 1958, since when she has been fitted with a further two new boilers. [KC]

No. 5 *Moel Siabod* poses at Clogwyn on 19th April 1963. No. 5 was built in 1896 (SLM Works No. 929) and named after a neighbouring mountain. She was also reboilered at Port Dinorwic and overhauled at Hunslets. [KC]

No. 6 *Padarn* poses in Llanberis station on 24th August 1961. No. 6 is the first of three of the later design delivered in 1922 (SLM Works No. 2838). Whilst of a very similar design to the first batch, these three locomotives are fitted with Schmidt superheaters (which reduce the tendency to prime) and the main visual difference is in the motion and the shape of the water tanks, with short side tanks but very deep well tanks providing greater overall water capacity. No. 6 was originally named *Sir Harmood* after the first company Chairman but had been renamed by 1924. [KC]

elevation would require the steam rack locomotives to work very hard indeed and soon wear out. But this is not the case as the locomotives were specifically designed for the task in question and are actually only in service for around half of each year. Most of their work is done with full regulator and a 60-80% cut off, which requires a fairly constant demand on the boiler and no particular uneven strains on the locomotive machinery.

After the First World War, traffic increased and so the rolling stock was augmented with further Swiss locomotives and carriages. During the Second World War, the line was requisitioned as radar development work was carried out in the summit hotel but traffic levels soon recovered in post-war years and demand for rides has continued, subject only to weather and the railway's capacity to carry increasing numbers of people.

However, understandably after some fifty years, heavy expenditure was soon required on almost everything: track, locomotives, carriages and the summit hotel. No. 4 *Snowdon* had been out of service since 1939 but, by 1963, it had been rebuilt, almost as a new locomotive, by Hunslets of Leeds and was back in traffic. Hunslets were used to Snowdon Mountain locomotives by now for, after some sixty years of service, most needed considerable attention. *Enid*, *Moel Siabod* and *Wyddfa* were all repaired by the firm. The carriages were rebuilt into closed and more modern looking vehicles. The Llanberis terminus station and facilities were

upgraded in 1960, resulting in increasing takings.

By and large, the Snowdon Mountain Railway was doing well, although traffic results depended on the weather and some years were better than others. Certainly, when compared with the newly emerging preserved narrow gauge railways, the mountain railway was prospering. The SMR was perhaps an anachronism in Britain as a commercially operated railway turning in profits. Over the last thirty years of the 20th century, almost every aspect of the railway was to be transformed as everything was beginning to feel its age and, in particular, much attention had to be given to the track. Indeed, for the latter part of the 1973 season, services were suspended above Clogwyn due to track defects. This, and having locomotives out of traffic for rebuilds and maintenance, restricted the services the company was able to run and so hindered its ability to run more trains to create the revenue to pay for the necessary upgrades.

This vicious circle was broken by the company being sold to Cadogan Properties in 1984. Through a Business Expansion Scheme share offer and with the aid of a Welsh Tourist Board grant, some £750,000 was raised to enable the railway to be modernised. Two rack-assisted diesel locomotives were ordered, track and passenger handling facilities were improved and the catering facilities upgraded. These steps were only just in time for, in 1984, the bogie of a carriage was derailed on the ridge above Clogwyn and, in 1987, No.7 ran away below the summit on a descending train; both

No. 8 *Eryri* poses on Llanberis shed on 19th April 1963. No. 8 was built in 1923 (SLM Works No. 2870) as the last of the three more modern locomotives and takes her name from the Welsh word referring to the whole of the Snowdon range – *'the abode of the eagles'*. It appears that No's 7 and 8 are today permanently out of service. [KC]

No. 8 *Eryri* waits at Clogwyn in company with another train on 19th April 1963. As there were no passengers on board, it can be presumed that the railway was only running to Clogwyn that day. [KC]

incidents fortunately were without loss of life or significant damage but were a warning received just in time.

The rack diesels cost nearly £2,500,000 each. Two arrived in 1986 and two more in 1991-92, all built by Hunslets of Leeds. They immediately proved their worth. The railway was now able to increase its services to cater for the passenger demand, almost instantly as required, being able to add trains into the service pattern to react to good weather and visibility. The diesels were able to make four daily return trips up the mountain, rather than the three trips by a steam locomotive. Soon half the services were operated by diesel. There was initially some resistance from passengers but, even so, demand for trips up the mountain outstripped supply of trains in the peak season. In 1984, 86,541 passengers were carried (which equates to 173,082 passenger journeys being the measure used by the preserved lines), 120,826 passengers in 1989 and, in the centenary year of 1996, 156,000 passengers with a turnover of £2,213,000 and a pre-tax profit of £227,000. The worth of the railway was further proved in 1998 when it changed hands once again, with Kevin Leech, who also owns Lands End and John O'Groats, buying the company for £1,300,000. The circle of improvements and additions to rolling stock continues, with more rack diesels and a specially promoted heritage rack-assisted steam train service. There is no reason why the Snowdon Mountain Railway should not continue to go from strength to strength. It fits the bill in providing an extraordinary experience and taking people to a unique part of the British Isles.

Halfway station is 1,641 feet above sea level and, as might be expected, is almost exactly halfway in distance between Llanberis and the summit station. It features a loop (the frame for which is seen here on 27th May 1987) and a watering point for steam locomotives. The line above Halfway changes in nature to become more obviously mountainous and steepens from 1 in 11 to 1 in 6^1/$_2$.

No. 4 *Snowdon* (SLM Works No. 988) descends over the ridge to Clogwyn on 20th September 1963. No. 4 was delivered in 1898 but was withdrawn in 1939 and virtually abandoned, being in a truly sorry state when the decision was made to send her to Hunslets in 1961 for complete reconditioning, taking two years. [KC]

No. 3 Wyddfa pauses at Halfway on 27th May, 1987 to take water whilst another up train powers up to Clogwyn and the summit of Snowdon seen in the distance.

In April 1971, a Down train runs over the Afon Hwch viaduct just above Llanberis, with one of the later series rack locomotives.

One of the original series of rack locomotives supplied by SLM blasts up the mountain above Halfway station on 27th May 1987, pushing one of the modernised carriages, converted to be completely enclosed.

Mountain trains pass at Halfway on 27th May 1987. Waiting in the station is No. 8 *Eryri*, one of the second series of SLM locomotives, as No. 3 *Wyddfa*, supplied to the line when it opened in 1895 (SLM Works No. 925), rounds the curve to take the loop with a train for the summit.

Close-up of No. 3 *Wyddfa*, paused at Halfway with an Up train on 27th May 1987.

In April 1974, No. 7 *Aylwin* (SLM Works No. 2869) is seen up on blocks with her wheels, axles and rack pinions, and wheels removed for maintenance in Llanberis workshops. In April 1978, its name was changed to *Ralph Sadler* (and ten years later shortened to just *Ralph*), to honour the former company engineer who did so much to improve the civil engineering on the railway. This locomotive appears to be permanently out of service.

Rack pinions and axles from No. 7 *Aylwin* in Llanberis workshops in April 1974. The rack pinions have fifteen teeth and when both are assembled together, they are staggered a whole tooth out of step. Each locomotive has two sets of rack pinions (one on each axle) and each set is half a tooth's difference in step from the other in order to give the surest grip and the best ride. Wear is inevitable and so the rack pinions are reversed every two years and replaced entirely every four years.

A complete wheel set, with axles and rack and pinion gear, from No. 7 *Aylwin* in Llanberis workshops in April 1974. Note the collar holding the axle on the wheel on the left, to enable the wheels to revolve freely (the locomotives are driven through the rack gear and not the rail mounted wheels) and the staggered double rack pinions in the centre either side of the brake drums.

An unidentified rack locomotive stripped to the frames for major overhaul in Llanberis workshops in April 1974.

Two spare boilers stand outside Llanberis station in April 1974. The boilers are set in the locomotive frames at an angle of 1 in 11, so that when the engine is working on the steeply inclined railway, the boiler is more or less level, needed to enable the water levels to cover both the boiler tubes and the firebox crown.

In June 1997, rack diesel No. 12 *George* rests at the Summit with the best view in the United Kingdom behind. Managing Director Derek Rogerson wanted the new diesels to have as distinctive a character as possible, so Hunslet was commissioned to deliver this, which they succeeded in doing by providing four rack diesels with exposed engines and revolving jackshafts. Rolls Royce engines were specified as most passengers would recognise the 'RR' on the bonnet. Four 320hp locomotives were delivered at a cost of nearly £250,000 each. No. 12, originally delivered in purple livery, was named *George* on 1st September 1996, after the Speaker of the House of Commons.

No. 8 *Fenella* on the last Peel train of re-opening day on 3rd June 1967, seen between Crosby and St. Johns. [David Mitchell]

SWASHBUCKLING SAVES THE ISLE OF MAN RAILWAY

6
SWASHBUCKLING SAVES
THE ISLE OF MAN RAILWAY

Like pretty much all narrow gauge railways in the United Kingdom, the Isle of Man Railway was in its dying throes, washed up and hung out to dry by the middle of the 1960s. Although it was a profitable company and still paying dividends, the railway, at least, was an outmoded transport system. Mr Sheard, General Manager since about 1930, seems to have been keen to keep the railway operating. But, by the 1960s it was wearing out; locomotives had to be taken out of service. It was his death, still in office, in mid-1965, which precipitated the closure. His successor, Bill Lambden, quickly found that the railway's revenue, and hence profitability, was being overstated. The contract for the school traffic was held by the railway and shown in its accounts but, by 1965, it was entirely carried out by the bus division of the company. Whilst traffic on the railway was initially suspended in November 1965 for urgent track repairs, the realisation about the school traffic income sealed the railway's fate. No trains at all ran in 1966. However, the Isle of Man Government were keen to see the railway kept going and the railway company obtained legislation to allow it to lease the operation to a third party ...

In 1967, there was much razamataz when all three lines from Douglas to Ramsey, Peel and Port Erin re-opened. The Marquess of Ailsa took a lease of the railway that April and clearly meant to show that the island's railways were still here to do business. His lease was for twenty-one years with the usual breaks at either seven or fourteen years. The first five years were, however, to prove enough even for the Seventh Marquess but his intervention was sufficient to buy the railway time for some sort of future to be worked out. Ailsa's intervention gave the necessary time for the Isle of Man Government to rethink its railway strategy and

The entire operating fleet of six steam locomotives, all freshly repainted in light green and adorned with flags, stand in Douglas station immediately before the opening on 3rd June 1967, sadly in wet weather. From left to right they are No. 15 *Caledonia*, No. 11 *Maitland* and No. 10 *G.H. Wood*, with No. 12 *Hutchinson* behind and, in the right background, No. 8 *Fenella* with No. 5 *Mona* behind. [David Mitchell]

No. 11 *Maitland*, freshly repainted in light green livery but as yet without the new crest, passes the signal box at St. Johns with a short train of four open wagons on a permanent way repair train on 30th May 1967, soon after the railway re-opened under the Ailsa regime. The train had reversed at St. Johns and was returning to Douglas. The wagons are empty and the gang will pick up old sleepers en route. Note the ladder placed on the signal box and what looks like fresh paint on the signal box woodwork. [David Mitchell]

The Isle of Man Railway was a complete system of three lines, two beginning at Douglas running to Port Erin and Peel (with simultaneous departures possible from Douglas) and the third branching off the Peel line at St. Johns (also with a branch from there to Foxdale). Apart from the Foxdale Branch, the system stayed intact into the Ailsa years with all its facilities. Here we see the goods yard at Douglas showing the freight transshipment facilities from rail to road. The photograph was taken in the spring of 1966 when the railway was closed; the goods wagons are stored and the lorries parked up. [David Mitchell]

then keep the south line to Port Erin open as a public steam railway with regular time tabled trains.

If you review the recent history of the Isle of Man Railway, all the books will tell you that the Isle of Man Railway was leased by the Marquess of Ailsa who put Sir Philip Wombwell in to manage it, that the operation was a financial disaster and the Marquess exercised his right in the lease to hand the keys back. But the history books do not tell you why the Marquess appeared on the scene or very much about him or Sir Philip; the story concentrates very much on the steam locomotives and the hive of activity on the railway during these times, extraordinary because only a year before the lease began the railway was closed as no-one was really using it apart from during the short summer holiday season. So, let's start at the beginning with the Ailsa family history.

On 7th April 1994, Archibald David Kennedy died at his home aged 68. His home was Cassillis Castle in Scotland and he was the seventh Marquess of Ailsa. He succeeded to the title in 1957 and his obituary recorded that he had a love of the sea and was a railway enthusiast; he had been a steam locomotive fireman, a soldier in the Korean War (as he was too old to serve as an officer), a director of the family's Ailsa Shipbuilding Company in Troon, had a steam model railway layout in the grounds of his Ayrshire home and once ran the Isle of Man Railway. So, we are just starting to peel the lid on the man and his make up. All these interests of the Seventh Marquess are relevant.

The family line began with the Earls of Cassillis and the twist in the tale lies with the eleventh Earl, who was created the first Marquess of Ailsa. Why? He was a sailor, known simply as Captain Kennedy of New York who fought in the Seven Years War. Whilst at sea he became friends with the Duke of Clarence, who was later to become King William IV, when he was serving as a midshipman also in New York. Kennedy's second son married the King's illegitimate daughter, Lady Augustus Fitzroy. Kennedy also made his fortune on prize money during the Seven Years War and profit he had earned from smuggling Portuguese bullion. Digging deeper, more money came into the family coffers following further smuggling on the Ayrshire Coast and an association with the Atlantic slave trade.

This was enough to fund subsequent generations betting £100,000 on a single horse race and losing the lot in one go (a very great deal of money at the time), squandering fortunes as notorious members of Fancy, the sporting fraternity of

Re-opening day poster, 3rd June, 1967. Although Ailsa had all the working locomotives repainted in light green, the poster perpetuates the earlier red livery.

the Regency, racing 40-ton cutters at sea and setting up a shipbuilding yard.

There is, as by now you can imagine, much more to this story but this is enough to set the scene for the Ailsa years on the Isle of Man Railway and perhaps explain, to some extent at least, the character and background to the Kennedys and their approach to life. Whilst supposition, it is probably not too far from the truth to consider that, for the seventh Marquess of Ailsa, taking a lease of the railway

The new Ailsa heraldic device photographed on 3rd June 1967, featuring No. 16 *Mannin* repainted in the new light green livery. The original IMR crest depicted one of the smaller locomotives but this was replaced by a red No. 16 sometime after the Second World War and then changed again to a green No. 16 by the Ailsa regime. [David Mitchell]

An Isle of Man lorry at Douglas station in spring 1966, loaded with luggage which has probably arrived in advance by steamer. It will be unloaded into the goods shed and then distributed around the island. [David Mitchell]

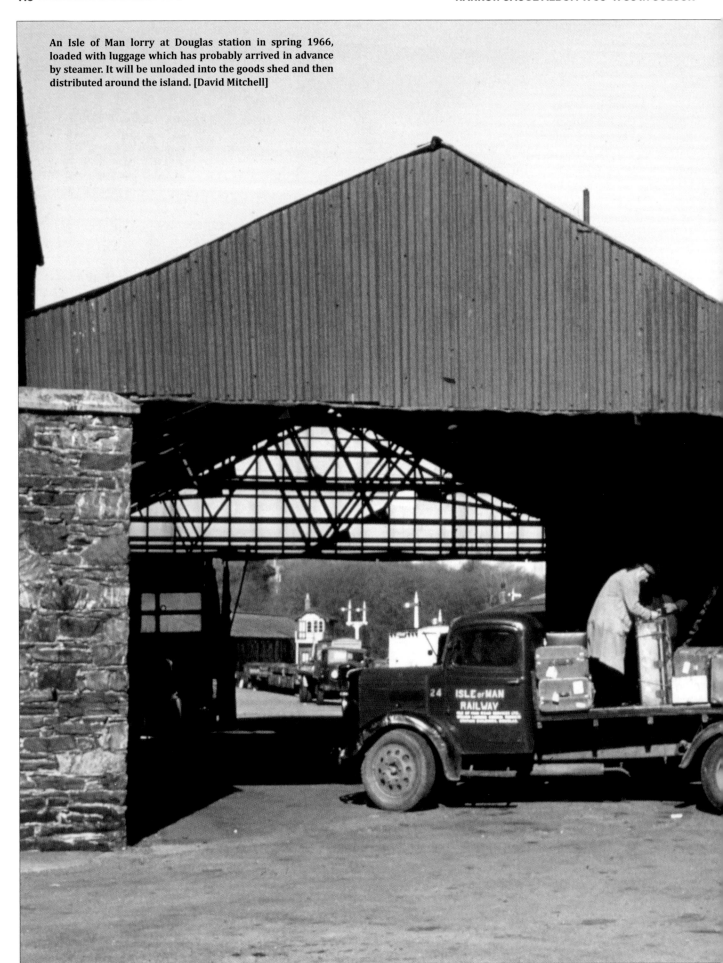

No. 11 *Maitland* hauls a short permanent way train between St. Johns and Crosby on 30th May 1967, shortly after re-opening. Some additional ballast has been laid on the track and the goods wagons are full of old rotten sleepers. [David Mitchell]

was akin to funding an enlarged train set simply because the opportunity arose and he wanted to take it. When compared to his predecessors exploits, his hobby was mild in the extreme. But Archibald David Kennedy was not born to do things by halves.

The Marquess appointed Sir Philip Wombwell (pronounced 'Woomwell') Bt as operating manager for the railway. This baronetcy is fascinating too. It was created for George Wombwell, Chairman of the Honourable East India Company and Member of Parliament for Huntingdon. The fourth baronet fought in the Crimean War and took part in the Charge of the Light Brigade but we digress ...

Ailsa made funds available to get the railway show back on the rails and brought some shipbuilding techniques into play, including specialised welding on the track to repair damaged or broken rails. Five of the Beyer, Peacock 2-4-0T steam locomotives were made fit for service: No. 5 *Mona*, No. 8 *Fenella*, No. 10 *G.H. Wood*, No. 11 *Maitland* and No. 12 *Hutchinson*, whilst with some effort, the former Manx Northern Railway 0-6-0T No. 15 *Caledonia* was also made useable; the two former County Donegal railcars completed the working fleet. Track and stock were repaired and staff re-employed with, most importantly, Locomotive Superintendent Donald Shaw being recalled from retirement; it is doubtful if the subsequent amazing operations would have been possible without his key knowledge. Ailsa ordered the steam locomotives to be repainted in a smart new light green livery, lined in black and white, and a new crest made depicting *Mannin* in the new green (modellers beware as the modern day crest has *Mannin* shown in red!). The re-opening day had all the useable locomotives in steam, decorated with multiple flags. Not content with smartening

up just the workable locomotives, from 1968, Ailsa had several of those in store put on show every day (and shunted into the carriage shed every night) at St. John's station, the junction on the Peel line for trains to Ramsey. These comprised No. 15 *Caledonia*, No. 16 *Mannin*, No. 6 *Peveril*, No. 1 *Sutherland* and No. 14 *Thornhill* (listed in the order in which they were displayed). And if that was not enough, on the recommendation of Sir Philip, who was concerned that there were not enough workable locomotives to operate the Ailsa service reliably, two new boilers were ordered from the Hunslet Engineering Company so that No. 4 *Loch* and, eventually, No. 13 *Kissack* could be returned to service after complete and thorough overhauls. Sir Philip apparently even tried, sadly unsuccessfully, to negotiate with Coras Iompair Eireann to buy the then redundant diesels from the closed Irish West Clare line. We should be eternally grateful to the Ailsa family sea faring 'traditions' for originally providing the capital for all this – a much more worthy cause than horse racing!

Ailsa determined to re-open the whole system, except the by now defunct Foxdale Branch (but one is given to wonder if he would not have run services over that too if it had been possible!). He was displeased about the installation of a new gas main between Castletown and Port St. Mary on the south line as this meant that, for the first season, services could only run as far as Castletown and not the full journey to Port Erin. The re-instated services were timed to start in June 1967 and not by half measures.

If running a railway, it might as well be run properly and Ailsa ensured Wombwell did that. A special for the Isle of Man Supporters Association was provided in the form of the two County Donegal Railcars visiting Peel and travelling as

No.11 *Maitland* with permanent way train in Douglas station on 30th May 1967 [David Mitchell]

The Seventh Marquess of Ailsa with the Island Governor, Sir Peter Stallard, walk behind the pipers and ahead of the Ailsa family on their way to the dais on the re-opening day at Douglas station. No. 10 *G.H. Wood* is alongside. [David Mitchell]

Locomotives galore at Douglas station on the re-opening day. No. 12 *Hutchinson* returns from Peel and is about to pass No. 8 *Fenella*, standing at the water column in the centre road, whilst No. 15 *Caledonia* is stationed in the goods yard on the right hand side of the carriage sidings. To the extreme right, wagons sit on the low level siding. [David Mitchell]

A surprise to many was the re-appearance of No. 15 *Caledonia* at the railway's re-opening ceremony on Saturday 3rd June 1967, newly repainted in green and bedecked with flags as station pilot. Here we see No. 15 shunting at Douglas station in the early afternoon, after the Directors' train had just returned. The Rev'd Teddy Boston had suggested the new light green livery to the Marquess and, in return, he was allowed to drive *Caledonia* on the opening day and his friend, the Rev'd Wilbert Awdry, was permitted to guard. Previously, *Caledonia* was very rarely seen in steam, having largely been retained for snow clearing purposes and it rarely snowed on the island. [David Mitchell]

No. 5 *Mona*, bedecked with flags on the re-opening day, stands after arrival at St. Johns with a train bound for Peel. Note the uniform carriage rakes; care had been taken with the trains to ensure matching carriage profiles. [David Mitchell]

No. 8 *Fenella* arrives at St. Johns with the last westbound train of the day to Peel, passing No. 10 *G.H. Wood* returning to Douglas on the re-opening day. Note that, by the afternoon, the weather had improved! [David Mitchell]

far as Kirk Michael on the Ramsey line on Sunday 28th May 1967. The next day, *Maitland* was busy shunting carriages in Douglas station in its new green livery. A double-headed, ten-coach train was even run from St. John's to Ramsey behind *Mona* and *Fenella*, presumably to see what happened after the line had lain fallow for almost a year; a most unusual working, including a number of former Manx Northern Railway coaches and resulting in a number of hot boxes on the bogies by the time the train reached Kirk Michael!

Sir Philip had planned a dramatic re-opening and, as he was a retired military man, he ensured that there was a dress rehearsal on Thursday 1st June. A cavalcade of steam locomotives was to parade down the centre release road at Douglas station and Sir Philip personally supervised the positioning of each locomotive.

News of all this had spread like wildfire on the railway enthusiast grapevine and two famous clergymen had got in on the act, bringing with them the new transfers of the revised heraldic device Sir Philip had ordered. The two men were to become an integral part of the staff for the opening, despite not having been trained or passed out on the railway; their pedigree and antecedent experience was enough. The Rev'd Teddy Boston owned the Cadeby Light Railway in Leicestershire and regularly drove his steam locomotive *Pixie* on it. The fact that the railway was in the Rectory garden and hardly amounted to 200 yards seemed to matter not at all. Teddy was rostered to drive *Caledonia* which was to be Douglas station pilot on the opening day. This was all

a bit of a surprise to the Isle of Man Railway 'watchers', as *Caledonia* had been kept much in the background and only really used for snow clearance for many years. Perhaps her Dübs Scottish ancestry appealed to Ailsa or, maybe, Teddy simply asked to drive her; he was that sort of person. He had suggested the revised railway livery and crest to Sir Philip and the very first locomotive to be painted in the new green livery was a 4mm scale model of an IoMR locomotive in Teddy's collection!

The second clergyman was none other than the Rev'd Wilbert Awdry, who had created 'Thomas the Tank Engine' and the 'Skarloey Railway.' He had done some guarding on the Talyllyn Railway so he knew what he was doing but not, of course, the IoMR's peculiarities. Although being reminded to screw the handbrake hard down on the run in to Peel and, despite his doing so, a train he guarded nearly ran into the stop blocks! Maybe, with hindsight, it was perhaps surprising Awdry did not write a children's story about the Isle of Man Railway.

The day after the dress rehearsal for the re-opening, the Ailsa family arrived at Ronaldsway airport and joined a special steam train for Douglas hauled by a flag bedecked *Maitland*, after Lady Ailsa had opened the new halt which only had its new nameboard and posts erected just in time; they had not been put up the day before! On arrival at Douglas, Sir Philip could be seen hurrying down the platform to meet the Marquess and his family to the accompaniment of a group of bagpipe players to add a Scottish flavour.

No. 15 *Caledonia* engaged in some carriage shunting, removing two carriages whilst No. 8 *Fenella* takes water in the centre road at Douglas station. The remaining four carriages formed the last train of the day with No. 8. The flags were removed from the locomotives once they had worked the re-opening specials and before they ran the afternoon trains. [David Mitchell]

No. 10 *G.H. Wood* starts out of Union Mills on the Peel line with the penultimate service train on re-opening day, passing another train on its way back to Douglas hauled by No. 5 *Mona*. [David Mitchell]

No. 8 *Fenella* pauses at Union Mills on the last train of the day to Peel. No. 8 was the only original small boilered locomotive working during the Ailsa regime, featuring the classic tall Beyer, Peacock tapered copper-capped chimney with brass numerals, which was to be seen on their locomotives exported all over the world. She was, however, withdrawn from service at the end of the following season. [David Mitchell]

In July 1967, trains pass at Port Soderick, the first station out of Douglas on the Port Erin line and one of the busiest on the network in the heyday of the railway. No. 12 *Hutchinson* is returning to Douglas and No. 5 *Mona* is arriving from Douglas. [David Mitchell]

The day before the opening had glorious weather but, sadly, Saturday 3rd June was damp and grey, although this did not detract from the proceedings. The platforms at Douglas were crowded with well wishers who were entertained by a brass band until the official party arrived. The island's Governor, Sir Peter Stallard preceded by Scottish pipers, led the party with the Marquess and his family up to the dais for the speeches. After the re-opening speeches, Teddy Boston had the honour of driving *Caledonia* to break the tape amidst a chorus of whistles from the other five locomotives, assembled behind, one on the centre road immediately behind *Caledonia* and two each on the platform roads by the buffer stops. They all then paraded up the centre road behind *Caledonia*. The re-opening train was hauled by *Maitland*. The leading coach in the train was No. F75, originally used by another Scottish gentleman railway enthusiast, the Duke of Sutherland, on the opening date in 1873; someone had done their research.

The re-opening train ran to Peel as a Directors' special. Three public trains, designated 'A', 'B' and 'C' also ran to Peel, following each other. Peel boasted the extraordinary sight of four steam locomotives and *twenty-seven* carriages all in the station at once! Public trains recommenced to Peel that afternoon, also behind *Maitland* and then to Ramsey on the following day. It was to be another month before trains ran on the south line but only as far as Castletown. Ailsa operated an intensive passenger service on all lines which tested the available motive power. The time table required all five workable Beyer, Peacock steam locomotives and the

railcars (which usually worked to Peel and Kirk Michael). *Caledonia* had to be pressed into service with a reduced boiler pressure to run some south line trains, after a head on collision at Union Mills which put two of the 2-4-0Ts out of service temporarily. Only Donald Shaw's intimate knowledge kept the service going at all.

During the first season of operation, an attempt was made to revive the Sunday specials to Braddan for the open air church services but the year of closure before Ailsa started up again had been enough for the coach companies to seize the business and so this plan never prospered. The endeavour was not assisted by one famous occasion when the driver, who was told to blow the locomotive's whistle at the end of the service, got the timing wrong and whistled up to the passengers to return to the waiting train whilst the Bishop was still mid-sermon. This caused several of the congregation to leave and the Bishop was reported as not being too pleased.

Not content with running a passenger service over all three lines, Sir Philip set to and won some freight traffic. He did a deal with the newly formed Isle of Man Ferry Express, which had set up its base in Castletown and competed with the long established Isle of Man Steam Packet Company. In the winter of 1967-68, the railway began a container freight service under the imaginative name of 'Man-tainor', using some second-hand British Rail containers. To run this, Sir Philip had the bodies of eleven of the 'pairs' coaches removed from their frames and burned. These were original 4-wheelers from the railways early days mounted on bogie

No. 12 *Hutchinson* prepares to leave Douglas station with a train for Peel on 22nd July 1968.

IoMR saloon No. F. 36 at Douglas. It had been pulled out of the works by No. 11 *Maitland*, where it had been overhauled for use by HM The Queen from Castletown to Douglas on 2nd August 1972. The directors and their wives are inspecting the carriage. The Isle of Man Railway had taken over operation in 1972. [David Mitchell]

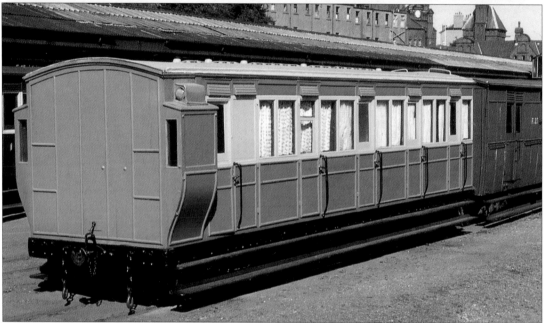

The Marquess of Ailsa had No. F.39, the Foxdale carriage, converted into a camping coach and painted blue and yellow. Seen here at Douglas in August 1968, it is not known if the carriage was ever used as such. [David Mitchell]

After being converted into a camping coach in 1967-68, full brake No. F. 39 was then used as a mess coach and the windows were boarded up for security, which enabled tools and equipment to be left inside. It was repainted in the standard colours of the time and is seen here at Douglas on 14th September 1978. [David Mitchell]

frames in pairs. The frames were converted into flat wagons and one further carriage was modified into a bogie well wagon. The trouble was that the service was doomed to failure from the outset. It incurred double handling costs at each terminal, the hire in costs of cranes from the UK and the fact that the ships were really designed to take modern sized ISO containers and not old wooden ones. The 'Man-tainors' proved logistically troublesome in every situation.

Other unusual freight workings were the oil and tomato trains! The railway ran oil tank wagons for the Isle of Man Electricity Board plants at Peel and Milntown, on the outskirts of Ramsey. This service began in the late summer of 1967, using three 'M' series wagons fitted with oil tanks and added to the rear of passenger trains and continued until just after the end of passenger services on the Ramsey line in 1968. No. 4 *Loch* just managed a trip there after being returned to service following reboilering in September that year. The tomato traffic ran using a passenger 'Empress' brake van (so called having been built in the year of Queen Victoria's Jubilee) from Castletown to Ramsey, via Douglas, where the van was stabled overnight. One night ,due to heavy rain and a leaking van roof, all the cardboard trays holding the tomatoes were spoilt; this led to the van being stabled inside the engine shed at night and then a 'G' type van being substituted.

Not surprisingly, the passenger and freight receipts failed to cover outgoings and so Sir Philip was asked to leave at the end of the first season after the 'Man-tainer' debacle and

Ailsa took over personally, although even he tried to extend that service to the Peel line but faced loading gauge obstacles.

Ailsa was obliged to spend a significant amount of money on rectifying the line to Port Erin following the pipeline being laid by the trackbed. The contractors had caused quite a lot of damage to the track and the drainage ditches, which took some time and money to repair. Ailsa always contended that he should not have had to spend this money as it was the railway company's responsibility; maybe this began to spell the beginning of the end as the operating costs were now a heavy burden and lateral settlement was to affect the formation for a number of years. Ailsa laid off staff and threatened to stop operating at all unless the lease was renegotiated for the 1969 season. The outcome of this was a release from the obligations of running trains on the Peel and Ramsey lines. With financial assistance of £7,500 a year from the Tynwald Government, trains continued to run just on the south line, now restyled 'The Victorian Steam Railway', with all the staff dressed in Victorian uniforms. Even George Crellin, the station master at St. John's, wore a top hat. Max Crookall was appointed manager for the 1969-71 period and worked hard to attract traffic. Traffic results did not improve, so Ailsa threw in the towel in March 1972.

The Government were still keen for the railway to continue to run as a tourist attraction so, with the same financial assistance provided to Ailsa, the railway company resumed operations and the line to Port Erin struggled on and even

The former County Donegal twin railcar set on a Douglas to Kirk Michael working, running beside the sea at Gob y Deigan on the Manx Northern line in July 1967. [David Mitchell]

No. 10 *G.H. Wood* runs by the sea at Glen Cam, just north of Gob y Deigan, on the way to Ramsey on 2nd June 1968. [David Mitchell]

Simultaneous departures from Douglas. The former County Donegal twin railcar set leaves for Kirk Michael, whilst a steam train departs for Castletown in July 1967. [David Mitchell]

The former County Donegal twin railcar set pauses in the drizzle at Kirk Michael on the Ramsey line on 28th May 1967. This was a special working on the weekend before re-opening, for the Isle of Man Steam Railway Supporters Association and ran from Douglas to Peel, then St. Johns to Kirk Michael and back to Douglas. [David Mitchell]

No. 5 *Mona* ready to leave Port Erin for Douglas on 22nd July 1968. This locomotive has not seen service since the Ailsa years but still exists, cocooned in the carriage shed, until the boiler asbestos coating is removed. *Mona* was provided with a larger boiler and side tanks, along with No's 4 and 6 in 1914. In 1978, No's 5, 7, 8 and 9 were sold to the Isle of Man Railway Preservation Society.

celebrated its centenary on Sunday 1st July 1973 (although technically it ought to have been a train on the Peel line, as that was the first line to open originally). A year later the opportunity was also taken to celebrate the centenary of the south line to Port Erin itself. For that occasion, *Loch*, also in her hundredth year, hauled the train which carried dignatories such as Sir John Paul, the island's newly-appointed Governor, also dressed in Victorian costume, meeting the Captains of the parishes and local people at each station. It was a shame that the Marquess of Ailsa was not there himself; he would have loved it.

Matters did not improve and in January, 1978 the railway company, once again, announced that it would no longer run trains. There was no option now but for the Government to buy the railway itself and set about re-organising and improving it to create the tourist railway it wanted.

Nameplate from No. 5 *Mona*, the ancient name for the Isle of Man. The unusual spacing of letters on both No's 4 and 5 was a result of the injector overflow pipe being extended down the tank sides and through a hole in the footplate. Unfortunately, the extended pipe bisected the nameplate so, instead of moving it forward on the tank, in order to maintain the symmetry, new plates were made with spacing between the letters to accommodate the pipe!

A carriage lamp photographed in July 1974.

Slotted signal in July 1974.

No. 11 *Maitland* returns from Ramsey to Douglas running by the sea south of Kirk Michael in July 1967. [David Mitchell]

On 14th September 1978, Isle of Man Railway ticket & information office carriage No. F9 sits on a temporary piece of track next to the short lived extension of the horse tramway system, to the sea terminal next to Douglas Promenade. [David Mitchell]

No. 12 *Hutchinson* leaves Douglas station with a train for Peel, passing No. 11 *Maitland* on shed on 22nd July 1968.

No. 11 *Maitland* on Douglas shed, August 1968. [PBW]

No. 12 *Hutchinson* having its smokebox cleaned alongside Douglas station on 22nd July, 1968.

No. 13 *Kissack* stands on shed behind two signals at the end of Douglas station platforms in July 1974. *Kissack* is a traditional Manx surname and No. 13 was named after Edward Thomas Kissack, who served on the railway board from 1902 to 1927. No. 13 is the fourth of the enlarged series of Beyer, Peacock locomotives which arrived in 1910. In 1967, Ailsa ordered two new boilers from Hunslets, for No's 4 and 13, although No. 13 was not so fitted until the winter of 1970-71.

In July 1974, No. 13 *Kissack* waits on Douglas shed for her next turn of duty, safety valves feathering.

No. 13 *Kissack* runs under the road bridge after leaving Sandton on her way from Douglas to Port Erin in July, 1974.

Port Erin locomotive shed and water tower in July 1974.

Ballasalla station in July 1974.

No. 13 *Kissack* uncoupling from her train after arrival at Port Erin with a train from Douglas in July 1974.

No. 1 *Sutherland* in the St. John's line-up in July 1974. The engine was named after the first Chairman of the railway company, the third Duke of Sutherland, a great advocate of railways, who was also a director of the London & North Western and Highland railways. No. 1's last season in traffic was 1964, although Ailsa attempted to steam her a couple of times so she could be used in the re-opening ceremony; sadly her boiler was simply not up to it but Ailsa put the locomotive in his stored line up anyway. Using No. 8's boiler, she was steamed for the railway's 125th anniversary celebrations in 1998 but is currently back in store. During the Ailsa years a line of static unused locomotives were put on display at St. Johns station each day whilst the Peel line was open (then moved to Douglas when only the Port Erin line remained open), displayed in the following order: *Caledonia, Mannin, Peveril, Sutherland* and *Thornhill*. The locomotive running the first train of the day to Peel dragged this line up out of the carriage shed every morning for display and they were put back under cover every evening. *Caledonia* is now part of the working fleet, whilst both *Mannin* and *Peveril* are on display in the museum in Port Erin goods shed.

No. 6 *Peveril* in the St. John's station line-up of stored locomotives in July 1974. In her working days, No. 6 was frequently outstationed at Peel and so became known as the 'Peel engine.' She has been mothballed since 1960, firstly put on display in the Ailsa locomotive line-up at St. John's and the subsequently at Douglas, and is now on show in the museum at Port Erin.

Saloon No. F30 sits in the centre road at Douglas in July, 1974.

'Pairs' coach at Douglas in July 1974, formed of two of the original four-wheeled carriages placed on a new bogie frames.

No. 13 *Thornhill*, built by Beyer, Peacock but for the Manx Northern Railway, stands at St. Johns in the Ailsa line-up of stored locomotives in July 1974. *Thornhill* was subsequently sold to a private owner on the island, Julian Edwards, and is not on public view.

No. 16 *Mannin* in the St. Johns station line-up in July 1974, repainted in the Ailsa light green livery, the only time this locomotive has ever been green. No. 16 arrived in 1926 and was ordered to meet the need for a larger locomotive to work the busy Port Erin linr, managing to take a twenty-two coach test train up Nunnery Bank within booked time. She spent most of her working life on that line, normally being outstationed there. Now, excitingly, there are plans to restore her to working order.

The Leighton Buzzard Light Railway (LBLR) was a 2ft gauge tramway serving extensive sand quarrying activities by two companies: George Garside (Sand) Ltd and Joseph Arnold & Sons Ltd, north of the town. Both were worked by Motor Rail & Tramcar Company Bedford-built, 4-wheeled, diesel-mechanical Simplex locomotives. For over forty years, Arnold's light railway carried sand from the quarries to the main line railway. This gradually decreased from the early 1950s, with road vehicle deliveries increasing, some directly from the quarries. The last sand train ran over the short remaining section of the LBLR on 2nd June 1981, from Churchways Quarry to the Eastern Way drying and grading plant. In this scene, at Churchways Quarry on 30th July 1970, George Garside's Motor Rail Simplex No. 34 *Kilmore* (Works No. 7105 of 1936) stands with a loaded train with No. 33 *Utrillo* (Works No. 7140 of 1936) behind. Both are 20/28hp class locomotives and named after notable winning racehorses. *Kilmore* was later re-named *Red Rum* and is now preserved by the Leighton Buzzard Narrow Gauge Railway Society but *Utrillo* was scrapped circa 1978. [Gordon Edgar]

7
ARNOLD'S SAND RAILWAY AT LEIGHTON BUZZARD

Laurie Brooks and Brian Harris, enthusiasts of American model railroads, decided they wanted to run a real railway following American practice and set out looking for equipment. In 1967, they arrived at Leighton Buzzard having heard about the 2ft gauge railway system carrying sand. They knew nothing about the history of the line but quickly stumbled across three sets of level crossings as they explored. Rather boldly, they simply decided that they would ask the owners if they could use it to run steam trains at weekends when it was not carrying sand. After all, Leighton Buzzard was in easy reach of London and this would save them the trouble of starting from scratch.

Laurie plucked up courage to ask the owner, a Mr Joseph Arnold, if it would be possible. Almost incredibly, Mr Arnold simply said yes! To begin with, there were none of the formalities which beset other preservation outfits. No

Light Railway Order, no Ministry inspection, no insurance, no safety management system or formal training. The volunteers simply got on with it. Of course, to start with, there were no locomotives, no carriages, no engine shed and no station either, just the enthusiasm of a new band of happy volunteers to run a railway.

It transpired that there were several other companies in Leighton Buzzard also running sand trains. Soon connections were made and the new team secured a shed from Garside as a temporary works. The fact that it was on the other side of the road from Mr Arnold's railway worried no one. When the volunteers secured four Simplex diesels at a price of £10 each from another operator, the St. Albans Sand & Gravel Company, they simply ran the diesels from the 'new' shed over the road cutting a neat double groove in the tarmac!

Word spread and soon quite a group of young volunteers

Chaloner, a de Winton vertical boiler locomotive, about to leave Pages Park station on the Leighton Buzzard Narrow Gauge Railway on 30th August, 1971.

Simplex petrol locomotive No. MR5612 departs from Pages Park at 10.45am with the first ever passenger train operated by the Iron Horse Preservation Society. The train comprised three of Arnold's ex-First World War 'D' Class bogie open wagons and ran the full length of the line to Double Arches and back on 3rd March 1968. [John Heys]

An hour later, a second train left Pages Park for Double Arches to cater for the high demand for rides on the inaugural day. Simplex No. 7 was borrowed from Arnolds for the day (including driver!), hauling two 'D' Class wagons. No seats were provided but, for once, a mobility impaired passenger had the advantage as his wheelchair was loaded in the leading wagon, so that he alone had the luxury of being able to sit down for the entire journey. [John Heys]

regularly appeared at Leighton Buzzard at weekends. It was great fun creating their own railway on an absolute shoestring. The diesels had a marvellous beat when their engines were turning over, smoke poured everywhere and several volunteers somehow found the smell of diesel fumes quite intoxicating. Running the diesels along the sand railway 'main line' was not for the faint hearted. The rails were quite buried in sand, some of the point blades were not connected to levers and were simply pushed over by foot to change direction. When a locomotive or wagon jumped the rails, the lads simply levered it back on again and carried on.

To formalise things just a little bit, on 15th October 1967, the Iron Horse Preservation Society was formed. The next step was to begin to promote the railway and an advert for a 'fan trip' was placed in the *Railway Magazine*. The trip would run over the entire length of the Leighton Buzzard Light Railway on 3rd March 1968 at a fare of 10s. Running a fan trip and issuing passes apparently overcame any necessity to involve the Railway Inspectorate or any other protocol! Mr Arnold seemed very happy and commented on the professional approach of the enthusiasts. The fan trip turned out to be three trips as so many people booked. A map of the sand railway system produced specially for the occasion showed Red Indians, Wells Fargo stagecoaches and horseback shoot outs!

John Heys, one of the early volunteers aged just fifteen, kept a diary of those days. He wrote about the opening day:

'*Sunday 3rd March 1968 dawned clear and bright. At a very early hour, many members assembled at the old Garside's shed at Billington Road. Two shops were set up, one by Laurie Brooks selling railway caps and badges and another selling refreshments. These were shortly joined by a Narrow Gauge Railway Society stand and an IHPS membership stall. Five of Arnold's bogie 'D' wagons had been brought down from Double Arches the day before, and had been stored overnight in the loops by the LBLR engine shed. Our Simplex MR5612, painted in a blue and yellow livery, was to be used, and a second loco was provided by Arnold's (No. 7). Passengers began to arrive in substantial numbers before 10am. About 100 were booked to travel, on one of the three trains timed to depart at 10.45, 11.45 and 15.00. Indeed, so many had asked for tickets that the 15.00 departure had to be added to the schedule just a few days earlier.*

The first train, consisting of 3 bogie wagons hauled by our MR5612 left roughly on time with Rod Hamilton at the controls. Those booked on the second train took photographs of the departure from a variety of vantage points. An hour later, the second train departed, with two 'D' wagons hauled by Arnold's No. 7 and driven by one of their staff. This was the first and last time since the railway's opening day in November 1919 that a

***Chaloner**, with Ken Brown driving, having arrived at Leedon Loop on a service train from Pages Park on 30th August 1971. At that time, Leedon was in the middle of fields but, within a few years, a housing estate had been built to the right of the photograph. There was a passing loop here so no hand shunting was necessary. The last passenger train of the day, however, was extended to Vandyke Junction, where there was a siding but no loop so hand shunting to position the locomotive on the front of the train was necessary. If the crew were lucky, the passengers helped with the shunting! [INSET] Chaloner's nameplate.*

The de Winton vertical boilered locomotive *Chaloner* being admired by a family whilst running round at Pages Park on 30th August 1971.

passenger train on the LBLR was hauled by a locomotive still in industrial service.'

The passengers on these trains were obliged to stand up inside the wagons, many holding on to each other for support, as the trains lurched down the uneven track to Double Arches.

The plan was to start public passenger trains that summer and, to this end, some effort was put in to improve the track in readiness. But the Society did not have a steam engine. However, Laurie Brooks had found out that there were quite a few individuals who had bought industrial narrow gauge steam locomotives and initially kept them at home. One such was Alf Fisher, who had rescued *Chaloner*, a vertical boilered steam locomotive from Pen-yr-Orsedd slate quarry in North Wales and had begun to restore this 1877-built antiquity at his home in Kings Langley. Laurie simply decided to call and ask if *Chaloner* could be used on the Iron Horse Railroad. Alf simply said yes too.

So the publicity began and initially majored on quite a few 'unique selling points', such as England's longest 2ft gauge railway and steam trains featuring *Chaloner*, the only de Winton vertical boilered locomotive under steam in the country. The Americanisation did not last very long though, promotion switching to refer to the Leighton Buzzard Narrow Gauge Railway Society.

The opening day was fixed for 29th June 1968 and

Chaloner was supposed to haul the inaugural train. Alf Fisher knew Teddy Boston, as Teddy's Bagnall 0-4-0ST *Pixie* was the first engine he had ever driven. The Rev'd Teddy Boston was renowned for his own 2ft gauge railway running in a 'U' shape round his rectory at Market Bosworth. He will reappear in several places in this book.

Once Teddy knew Alf had bought *Chaloner* he admonished him, saying *"What is the point of having a steam engine which doesn't go anywhere!".* So Alf felt obliged to invite Teddy to the opening day. *Chaloner* had not moved under her own power for fourteen years, so a test run was the order of the day but not until the opening day itself! Alf and Teddy were on the footplate as they set off to go to Standbridge Road and back to see what happened hauling one carriage. *Chaloner* struggled on the bank and Alf thought the train would not make it but Teddy was made of sterner stuff and far more optimistic: *"Where's your faith, lad?".*

Alf takes up the tale: '*Naturally the old girl heard about this divine intervention and immediately picked up speed and we rolled along without a problem until we went over Stanbridge Road crossing with a loud bang and an unnatural rumble. On the return, the Rev'd 'Teddy' was in the driving seat and Stanbridge Road again became a hazard as she stuck fast in the middle of the road.* "Set back and take a run at it" *were the pearls of wisdom I gave him. He certainly did, and he got*

P.C. Allen prepares to depart from Bryan's Loop, between Vandyke Junction and Henley Hill Road, in July 1971. The last train each day was extended beyond the normal destination at Leedon to provide extra interest. Bryan's Loop has since been removed. *P.C. Allen* is an Orenstein & Koppel 0-4-0WT built in 1913 (Works No. 5834) for the internal railway system at the Spanish chemical works of Solvay & Cie, in Torrelavega. It was purchased in 1963 by Sir Peter Allen, Chairman of ICI, who wrote many railway books in association with PBW. [John Heys]

over the crossing in fine style but was still going a cracking pace when he hit the points leading to the concrete works at the other side of the road where he hit the deck. Moreover a huge jolt in the middle of the road had loosened all the fire bars which were now in a smouldering heap of ashes between the tracks, some even on the road itself.'

The inaugural train was due to leave Pages Park shortly but *Chaloner* was not going anywhere! However, she was quickly rerailed and ran fireless back to Pages Park where the firebars were reassembled and the fire relit. Wisdom had prevailed and

the inaugural train, complete with Carnival Queen, left diesel-hauled. But *Chaloner* did get a trip out on the first day on a passenger train. The diesel set out with three carriages but returned with only two, having struggled to get up the bank and left one carriage and passengers marooned at the foot of Footbridge bank. *Chaloner* went out on a rescue mission and returned triumphant with her first passenger train ever!

From hereon, the Society really got into its stride and progressed from having a weekly whip round to buy coal for *Chaloner* to operating regular steam hauled services.

The Leighton Buzzard Narrow Gauge Railway right of way on 30th August 1971.

Garside's No. 27 hauls a heavily loaded sand train out of Munday's Hill Quarry, headed for Double Arches on 21st September 1971. [John Heys]

George Garside's Motor Rail Simplex No.17 *Damredub* (Works No. 7036, built in 1936) on the 'main line' with empty silica sand skips outside the Double Arches dryer and grading plant on 30th July 1970. The locomotive was probably working from Munday's Hill Quarry. This is the intersection of Mile Tree Road and Eastern Way, and the finger post sign points off right to Watling Street and left to Heath & Reach. Just look at the sand on the road from HGV vehicles using the plant. Beyond the level crossing, the railway track forked left to Joseph Arnold's works, and right to George Garside's, and the latter company's sign can be seen on the brick building. The Eastern Way installation came into use in 1965 and received sand from Munday's Hill Quarry, which was coarse white and brown, and from Churchways Quarry, which was fine grade. The Simplex is now preserved on the Leighton Buzzard Light Railway. The overgrown track has been cleared to this point during 2018, as the railway wishes to relocate its heritage workshops here from Stonehenge. [Gordon Edgar]

Garside's 20hp Simplex No. 34 *Kilmore* crossing Eastern Way at Double Arches on 21st September 1971. [John Heys]

A scene on 30th July 1970, with a rather oily George Garside's Motor Rail Simplex 4-wheeled, diesel mechanical No. 33 *Utrillo*, heading a loaded sand train from Munday's Hill Pit for tipping at the Eastern Way drying plant, running alongside the Miletree Road. [Gordon Edgar]

The Doll, an Andrew Barclay 0-6-0T built in 1919 (Works No. 1641) at Bressingham on 23rd July 1967, before transfer to Leighton Buzzard in 1972. [KC]

Garside's No. 34 *Kilmore* about to cross over Eastern Way as it departs from Double Arches on 21st September 1971. [John Heys]

A general view of Arnold's sand plant at Double Arches, with no fewer than five 20hp Simplex petrol locomotives in action on 21st September 1971; from left to right they are No's 18, 30, 4, 14 and 33. [John Heys]

Arnold's Simplex No. 18 waiting under the sand grading plant, with No. 14 on a train of empty skips in the background on 21st September 1971. [John Heys]

Pixie, a Kerr Stuart 0-4-0ST built in 1922 for Devon County Council (Works No. 4260), on shed at Pages Park on 30th August 1971.

8
RISHRA

PART 1: MIKE SATOW

Shortly after the turn of the last century, the firm of E.E. Baguley Ltd was established in Burton on Trent. Prior to establishing his own company, Major Baguley worked for a number of years with Bagnalls and was the draughtsman responsible for their range of small industrial saddle tank locomotives. Two features characterized his locomotives: the 'bull head' boiler, with its cylindrical firebox, and his radial valve gear in its original and modified versions.

Until the end of the First World War, Baguleys concentrated on internal combustion engines for their motive power, producing a range of railcars and trolleys which found their way to many improbable corners of the world. In 1919, Baguley embarked on the production of small steam locomotives, available in five cylinder sizes and various gauges. These engines had much in common with earlier Bagnall machines but carried water in side tanks rather than saddle tanks. They were known, rather loosely, as the 'Flanders' Class and, although only seventeen were built, they found their way to many remote places in the wake of their petrol engine brethren.

Our story is now concerned with No. 2007, the sole survivor of the two smallest engines of the class. No. 2007b was laid down for stock in 1919. She was built for 2ft gauge and, in common with the rest of the class, was fitted with Baguleys modified valve gear, a form of radial gear employing anchor links in a reversing yoke in place of the expansion link and die block of his original design. Both these gears give constant lead at all points of cut off.

In August 1921, Baguley received an order from Light Railways Ltd of London (order No. 903 24/8/1921) for: '*One Flanders standard 0-4-0 side tank locomotive No. 2007... the boiler must comply strictly with the Bengal Boiler Act ... to be suitable for burning Bengal coal ... packed in a substantial*

Rishra **with the Narrow Gauge Railway Society's special train on 30th June 1973.**

timber case.' On 28th November 1921, the packing case was consigned to Calcutta Corporation, ending its journey at the Pulta pumping station in Barrackpore, whence Calcutta's dubious water supply still emanates. This was in 1921 and marks the end of the early history of what must be the smallest industrial steam locomotive ever to be exported from Britain.

Forty-two unrecorded years must pass before I found myself exploring the 'industrial archaeology' of the Pulta pumping station on a hot Sunday afternoon in March 1963. The most notable feature of the waterworks was the extensive network of narrow gauge track, which seemed to connect everything and everywhere but which obviously served the primary purpose of bringing coal from the river bank to the boiler house. Inquiry about locomotives brought the discouraging reply that there were none – and never had been – and that the coal and ash were propelled to and from the boiler plant by man power. This was a convincing enough statement in 1963 Bengal; but driving out past the maze of 'branch' lines, there was a lurking feeling that when the British Raj laid railway lines, they usually put a locomotive on them. Vigilance

was maintained and finally rewarded when, down the second branch on the left, a clothes line was sighted with one end tethered to a tree, the other wound round something which might have come from the pen of Emmet.

Just how long No. 2007 had been reduced to supporting a clothes line remains a mystery. She must have been standing there, overgrown with 'jungle,' rotting away as each monsoon swept over her, for some twenty-three years. She was a sad sight. The side tanks and all the other light sheet metal had rusted away, all removable copper and brass had disappeared, and the rest was rusted solid. I had, at that time, no idea of her age or origin but the 'bull head' boiler and the unusual valve gear stood out as distinctive features. I tore away at the enveloping vegetation and was about to photograph the interesting details when an armed sentry intervened and reminded me that the use of cameras was forbidden on Government property. Now I am always pleasantly surprised when I find my photographs have turned out well but I was astonished to find some excellent exposures of an apparently identical locomotive and its unusual valve gear when the film was developed! Prints were despatched with a request for identification to a certain Mr (then) Peter Allen, who happened to be a Deputy Chairman of the company for which I worked. He kindly passed them round a number of knowledgeable friends and finally I received a reply from one of them who identified the engine as one of Baguley's.

Until then I had not been particularly interested in railways but my interest in this forlorn but fascinating relic was growing. I decided that a rescue operation and subsequent rebuilding might enliven the course of our engineering apprentices at our Rishra factory. After all, a bit of real machinery is more exciting to work on than filing square holes to fit round pegs, so we opened negotiations with Calcutta Corporation for the purchase of the engine.

We offered book value, scrap value, even a new clothes post but a year went by with no sign of progress. We offered them a maintenance contract at Rs 5s per annum, coupled with a penalty clause that we would pay a lump sum equal to its book value if we did not return it to them in working order

within three months. Accepted! And so, one day in 1964, No. 2007 was dug out of the undergrowth by a gang of apprentices, loaded onto the back of a lorry, and set out towards a new life. The first, but only the first, hurdle had been cleared.

While these negotiations were in progress, I visited Baguley's factory in Burton on Trent, in search of historical and technical information. The late Mr F.C. Souster, then Managing Director of the firm, dug out no less than forty-seven original drawings which he presented to me with the remark: "*We don't seem to have had a repeat order since 1921 so I don't think we'll need them again!*". I became the owner of the design and goodwill of Baguley 4in. x 8in. 'Flanders' Class.

Back in Calcutta, the engine had been stripped to the frames. The boiler was a problem, because, although it seemed generally sound, there was a heavily corroded area on the outside front shell where rain, dripping from a tree, had almost penetrated the plate. We sent for the boiler inspector and tripped over the next hurdle. He, it seemed, could only inspect the boiler if requested by the owners. We were not the owners. He also pointed out that the employment of apprentices on repairs to 'mobile' boilers was prohibited by the regulations. This was a mobile boiler. I can only say that we ended up with a new front shell on the boiler, new tubes, and a certificate for operation at its original pressure!

Time was passing, and my own time in India was drawing to a close. By March 1971, two months before my departure, No. 2007, jacked up on blocks for want of any track, came to life and turned her wheels with her own steam. Eight years had passed since I first saw her and I was becoming somewhat attached to her. My offer to buy her and take her to England to continue her working life was accepted with less prevarication than in 1963 but there was a risk that an expatriate leaving India with a steam locomotive amongst his

personal effects might arouse suspicion, if not incur delay. I left her behind but shortly after my arrival in England an order was received in India for a locomotive suitable for working on the 2ft gauge line of the Leighton Buzzard Narrow Gauge Railway Society. Baguley No. 2007 was once again confined to a substantial timber case, a letter of credit for the purchase price was opened and she was loaded into the hold of SS *Jala Jawhar* consigned to Liverpool, freight forward.

She must have been somewhere off the coast of Africa when a letter came from Calcutta saying that I should not pay the freight on arrival in Liverpool until I received further instructions. These came when she was somewhere off Holyhead and told me to pay only half the amount quoted. '*This would have covered a new locomotive*', the letter read, '*For yours, being very old, we have negotiated a 50 per cent reduction.*'!

In November 1971, for the second time in her life, she emerged from her packing case, mechanically sound, far from complete, and completely unrestored. I stripped her right down, examined everything and listed every item of work, awarding priorities and classifying work as 'home' or 'away' (Leighton Buzzard). This was necessary, because I lived 200 miles from there, and everything except the frames, wheelsets, boiler, tanks and cab had to be loaded into the car and taken home for attention. Working to the priority list, items were overhauled, new parts were made, and all was polished or painted before return to Leighton Buzzard in time to fit in with a normal rebuilding sequence. Only the heavy assembly work, lagging (timber), casing of the boiler and final painting was carried out at Leighton Buzzard. Painting and lining were done as nearly as possible to the original livery, a small patch of the original bronze green having survived under many layers of grime in a sheltered corner of the footplate. New patterns and castings were made to replace the mutilated base of the smokestack and the missing sandbox cover, and all was done in conformity with the original drawings.

The result has been a great reward for many years of frustrating negotiation and the 650 hours – almost equally divided between 'home' and 'away' – spent bringing her back to original condition. There were many doubts, when she reappeared in England, as to whether she would be capable of any useful work on the heavily graded track at Leighton Buzzard but she has shown herself capable of handling nine tons up 1 in 28, with the boiler making steam in the process! The only serious problem is that everything is very near the ground and gets covered in sand. Guards, fitted between the front brake blocks and the crosshead guides, have effected an improvement, and the next step is to convert the motion to grease lubrication.

Unnamed until 1972, she now carries the name *Rishra* as a token of gratitude to the several generations of apprentices from the works at Rishra who achieved her rescue.

Rishra in the siding at Munday's Hill.

8
RISHRA

PART 2: PETER LEMMEY

On 30th June 1973, I arranged for the Narrow Gauge Railway Society's London area to hire a train for the afternoon on the 2ft gauge Leighton Buzzard line in Bedfordshire. It was a sunny summer Saturday, there were seventeen passengers and we were hauled by their little Baguley 0-4-0T *Rishra*. It was not a particularly ambitious run – we can't have travelled more than six miles all afternoon – but it was nonetheless highly enjoyable, and is still warmly remembered by those who took part. That it was so memorable an outing says a lot about the Leighton Buzzard line, and something too about what it was like to be a narrow gauge enthusiast in the 1970s.

For our 30th June 1973, trip we arrived at Pages Park on the outskirts of the town, then as now the starting point for Leighton Buzzard Narrow Gauge Railway services – to find *Rishra* in steam beneath the trees, ready to take our two-coach train up the line. At the time of our visit the vertical boiler de Winton 0-4-0 *Chaloner* and Kerr, Stuart 0-4-0ST *Pixie* were also in service, while the Orenstein & Koppel 0-4-0T *PC Allen* and Andrew Barclay 0-6-0T *Doll* were being overhauled. It is illustrative of the LBNGR's early years that the railway was relying on lightweight 0-4-0Ts to work its passenger trains and that there was yet no public service on Saturdays: we had the railway entirely to ourselves.

Many narrow gauge enthusiasts coming of age in the 1960s and 1970s were drawn to volunteer on individual railway preservation schemes, for many a life-long connection. However, there was also an overlapping population of railway enthusiasts with a more general interest in the narrow gauge world, and for them organisations like the Narrow Gauge Railway Society provided a way of getting in touch with like-minded members, sharing historical research and keeping up with new developments, albeit mostly on the preservation scene. Yorkshire enthusiasts had started the

Rishra at Pages Park waiting to set off up the line with the NGRS special on 30th June 1973, providing a good view of her cab layout, and marine boiler and firebox. The couplings are simple links and the only brake is the handbrake.

Rishra being cautiously driven over the points at Munday's Hill, watched by Andy Muir holding the point lever.

Society in 1951, with a number of original members having worked for Leeds locomotive builders. The NGRS had grown steadily under the leadership of Ron Redman (who had been with Hudswell, Clarke & Co.) and published a regular newsletter and a journal distributed to members all over the country. In a number of cities members had set up Society area groups with programmes of monthly meetings: our London area group was one of them.

There had been a London area group of the NGRS since the late 1950s and by the early 1970s the group was under the benevolent oversight of Donald Boreham. In the 1960s, the London area had been responsible for much good work in preserving the Fletcher, Jennings 0-4-0T *Townsend Hook* and other industrial locomotives, and in driving the Brockham Museum project which much later mutated into Amberley. In due course, Donald widened the London area's focus to include narrow gauge modelling (he was a member of the Merioneth group) and he also encouraged us to look at railways abroad. Although French narrow gauge had largely disappeared by the 1970s, London talks by John Snell kept memories of the metre gauge *Secondaires* alive, while slide shows by D. Trevor Rowe on topics like narrow gauge steam in Saxony showed what was still active further afield. In some ways we narrow gauge enthusiasts seemed as well informed about some of the narrow gauge across the Channel as we were about developments at home: the primer had been

Bryan Morgan's *The End Of The Line* but we had also watched the *Railway Roundabout* TV films about European railways by Patrick Whitehouse and John Adams. W.J.K. Davies's *Light Railway Notes* which appeared monthly in *Railway World* and ranged from Portmadoc to Port Shepstone had also become required reading. And of course a dawning awareness of Britain's railway legacy in India had been given a focus by the return of *Rishra*.

In early 1973, two friends who volunteered at Leighton Buzzard suggested the idea of a London area special train. It was through a notice in *Narrow Gauge News*, the NGRS's national newsletter, that we recruited our seventeen bookings, charging 70p a head and neatly filling two coaches. In those days, before the internet or Facebook, society newsletters and periodicals were one of the main ways to contact other enthusiasts about such outings. While these society publications covered plenty of railway history, up-to-date news of the latest narrow gauge activity was often a bit haphazard, mainly dependent on a random flow of reports from individual society members rather than on the regular press releases which keep us in the picture today. Railway preservation as on the Leighton Buzzard line was still pioneering work and even enthusiasts living quite locally could be unaware of developments: I think few if any of the NGRS members on our train had visited the Leighton Buzzard line before – unsurprising perhaps for participants like John and Anne Browning who had come down from Yorkshire but for us Home Counties members it was mostly new track too. Our expectations for the day were based mainly on what we had read or picked up from others; but we had heard enough to be drawn by the promise of narrow gauge steam in surroundings both rural and industrial, by seeing a Baguley engine in steam ... and for some of us at least the promise of grass between the rails in true light railway fashion. We were not to be disappointed.

Our train left Pages Park heading along the 2ft gauge main line with *Rishra* running cab first. The railway's Clive Gibbard was at the regulator. The engine ran smoothly all day, and Clive and the crew took the photo-stops and run-pasts in their stride: their friendliness and informality was a feature of the journey. Our flagmen that day included the young Andy Forbes, hardly even a teenager, and he was kept busy at the various ungated road crossings. Taken up as we were with enjoying the day, few of us gave much thought to what the future promised for the railway: it wasn't obvious that the fields and meadows which we were running through would soon be developed for housing, nor that increasing passenger traffic would soon mean that *Rishra* and her 0-4-0T sisters would become too small to work the regular trains.

On our trip that Saturday, Mundays Hill was as far as we went. Here *Rishra* was uncoupled and ran onto a spur, perhaps part of the loop (it was all too overgrown to be sure), while the train crew hand-shunted our two coaches past the engine. *Rishra* then coupled up again on the other end ready to haul us back smokebox first. The first stop on our return journey was at Stonehenge workshops. There we were shown the LBNGR's growing collection of 2ft gauge industrial diesel and steam power: a chance, too, to chat to other passengers, put faces to names and to spark friendships which continue to this day. Then it was back on board behind our little 0-4-0T and off in the direction of Pages Park, with on the way several more photo-stops, a couple of run-pasts and some careful negotiation of the level crossings, the young Andy flagging us over. Leaving Leedon Loop, *Rishra* took us steadily up the 1 in 25 climb to Stanbridge Road, and then all too soon we were back at Pages Park.

Over the ensuing years both the Leighton Buzzard Railway and the Narrow Gauge Railway Society have thrived in ways undreamt of in 1973. However, it is good to recall our NGRS trip from time to time and be reminded of what being a narrow gauge enthusiast was like then, and of the fun we had on that Saturday afternoon.

Rishra **and the NGRS special train on the return journey on 30th June 1973. Note the members' attire – London Area Secretary, Peter Lemmey in brown jacket and flares, and other members in jackets and ties.**

The track layout at Munday's Hill was set out to suit quarry operations, with no need for a run round loop. So in order to run round her train, *Rishra* pulled forward, reversed into a siding, then the train crew (Derek Trevellion, Andy Muir and Clive Gibbard) pushed the coaches beyond the siding point so that *Rishra* could couple up to the front for the return trip. [Peter Lemmey]

9
SOLD DOWN THE RHEIDOL

In May 1971, No. 9 *Prince of Wales* stands in Aberystwyth station with a short four-coach charter train specially prepared for PBW to take pictures which appeared in the short lived '*Steam Alive*' quarterly magazine published by Ian Allan. [PBW]

As long ago as 1962, the then British Railways Western Region Chairman, Reggie Hanks, well known for supporting steam and who had managed to outshop the last Class '9F' in BR lined green with a copper capped chimney, spoke regretfully about the Vale of Rheidol line: "*I fear the days of the very attractive little railway are numbered.*" But he was also realistic, albeit ahead of his time and suggested that the line might be sold for volunteers to run following the success of both the Talyllyn and Festiniog Railways. He was instrumental in helping Pat Garland and Pat Whitehouse choose GWR 'small prairie' tank No. 4555 for preservation in main line operating condition and no doubt the three men will have discussed the Rheidol as, of course, the two Pats had cut their preservation teeth on the Talyllyn.

So it probably was not too much of a coincidence when, in 1969, Mr Robert Lawrence, Chairman and General Manager of the London Midland Region, invited Pat Whitehouse for lunch and asked him "*if it would be possible for a large enough group of individuals to band together and raise sufficient capital to purchase the Vale of Rheidol line from British Rail*

and so decently get them out of the problems and costs which must arise if BR have to continue to run an isolated short length of steam railway.".

Pat enlisted the 'Who's Who' of railway preservation: Pat Garland, Sir Peter Allen, Brian Hollingsworth, Geoff Drury, Dickie Dunn and John Snell, the latter being the keenest and who led the charge. By August 1969, Snell had formed a company and, by December in the following year, he had imported two East German 0-8-0 tender locomotives, one being sent to the Festiniog and the other to Carnforth for assessment and storage. Snell became the principal activist in this venture. He had previously discussed the prospect in 1967 with George Dow, Divisional Manager BR at Stoke, who had the unenviable task of managing the VoR within his empire but a task he relished. All these men knew each other as friends and all of them were members of the rather exclusive Grand Junction Club, which met twice annually for a black tie dinner at the Midland Hotel in Birmingham where, over a glass or two of claret, all manner of possibilities were often discussed and several put into practice.

George Dow was in favour of keeping the Rheidol alive and

No. 9 *Prince of Wales* hauls a fully loaded train painted in the short lived Cambrian Railways green livery and branded 'VoR', at Troedrhiwfelen. Note the coal on the locomotive has been piled up out of the top of the bunker around the safety valve bonnet.

had fought valiantly and successfully for its cause. In the post war 1950s, the 2ft gauge line remained within the Western Region's ambit and was cosseted by Oliver Veltom, Assistant Divisional Manager at Chester and with some success. The three GWR 2-6-2Ts and all the carriages had been repainted in BR (WR) express train livery of lined green for the locomotives and chocolate & cream for the carriages and, with enhanced publicity, passenger numbers had risen, although still not in the same league as the embryonic Talyllyn and Ffestiniog reincarnations further up the Welsh coast. However, in 1963 the Beeching Report was published which included instructions about dispensing of redundant assets and disposing of recoverable assets. This translated into the loss of passing loops at both Capel Bangor and Aberffrwd, the closure of intermediate halts and the closure of Aberystwyth shed and led to rostering for the VoR being moved to Machynlleth. The line itself was transferred to be within the management of the Stoke Division and under the capable leadership of George Dow, probably then also the leading authority on the Great Central Railway's history. Dow was an experienced railwayman and certainly knew how to get things done. Being enthusiastic, he lost no time in inspecting his new

BR time table poster from 1969 showing the return fare at 10s.

steam railway and he was to prove pivotal in saving its life. First, he ordered several improvements: renovating Devil's Bridge station, adding 'height above sea level' details to station and halt nameboards and, somewhat controversially, the repaint of the entire fleet of locomotives and carriages in BR blue, complete with 'double arrow' logo.

Dow then proposed a scheme to move the narrow gauge Aberystwyth station into vacant platforms in the standard gauge station, eliminating the level crossing, and moving the locomotives and carriages into the then redundant main line engine shed. This proposal would have cost £5,000 and, when it came to the ears of his superiors in Euston, they turned the scheme down and, worse, ordered the line to be sold as they then realised the line ran at a loss. Heads had been raised too high above the parapet, although not for the first time. There had been some encounters with trying to sell the VoR before, resulting in discussions with the likes

of the local council and even the National Trust, but all to no avail. Dow bought time by convincing authority that, if the line was to be sold, a proper valuation should first be carried out.

Luck was with George Dow. He came to hear that Barbara Castle, the then Minister of Transport, was to visit Aberystwyth on 1st July, 1967 to address a Labour Party rally. He lost no time in adding a trip down the VoR into her itinerary and suggested to her during her ride that the Rheidol line was a splendid asset to BR and the Welsh tourist trade and that it should neither be sold or closed! She agreed and he got approval to implement his £5,000 improvement scheme!

But BR had not forgotten and head office smarted and plotted. Hence the lunch between Lawrence and Whitehouse, which they hoped would settle the game once and for all. But matters did not turn out immediately as BR wished and it was not to be until 1988, some twenty years later, before they would be able to divest themselves of this line which irritated the top brass so much.

Snell was largely left to lead the preservation charge. He wrote: *'It would be appalling if public money was used to prop up a lacklustre operation when an independent and local management could run the line without leaning on the taxpayer. This is no criticism of British Railways: they are, after all, providers of transport and this railway is a provider of entertainment. The answer seems to be that the railway should be taken over by a company backed by the money of enthusiasts and well wishers. The line has never been a gold mine and never will be; but it seems clear that if it is put on its feet and run with energy and local knowledge it can sustain itself financially and be a much greater asset to the district than it has been latterly. This is the proposal now being put forward. It is difficult to see what other possibility there is.'.*

In 1970, the Conservative Party won a surprise victory in the general election, ousting Harold Wilson's Labour party. Government and the unions had begun to grow apart in the 1960s and Heath pledged to tackle union power and introduced the Industrial Relations Act which was challenged by the unions, who saw it as restricting

No. 8 *Llywelyn* approaches Quarry Cutting on the final climb into Devil's Bridge.

No. 8 *Llywelyn* takes water at Devil's Bridge on 18th December 1988, the last day of BR operation. Painted in Cambrian Railways dark green (nearly black to the naked eye), the locomotive carries a wreath signifying the end of British Rail service.

their freedom to negotiate. Heath tried to keep wages and inflation down but was bedeviled by a successful miners' strike, showing great unity in preventing coal from reaching power stations, resulting in power cuts. Snell, himself an arch Conservative and later Thatcher supporter, had perhaps not reckoned sufficiently with the power of the unions in railways, preferring to rely on his economic logic. The ASLEF Union got to hear of the preservation scheme. It was not difficult for them to do so, or to see the angle being taken by them as well, as Snell was vociferous in continuing to publicise his cause in the railway press: '*The professionals of BR could not bring themselves to admit that they could not match the performance of these 'amateur' railwaymen, when the potential tourist attraction of the Rheidol line was certainly no less than the others.*' Whitehouse and Garland were happy enough for Snell to take the lead and indeed all the honours, if there were to be any, as they then had their hands full with the Dart Valley Railway plc and Whitehouse had even branched out into possessing the last Western Region 'Castle', which was to keep him well occupied together with trying to convince BR to overturn the ban they had imposed in 1968 on steam locomotives being used on their system. Hollingsworth was building a $7^1/_4$ins line in the Welsh mountains, Drury had acquired two L&NER 'Pacifics' and Dunn was inextricably involved with the Severn Valley Railway. Was Snell being hung out to dry?

ASLEF enlisted the support of local politicians and, by 1972, the Vale of Rheidol was once again not for sale. Snell repatriated both the German locomotives he had imported and, instead, concentrated successfully on managing the Romney Hythe & Dymchurch Railway, rebuilding it to much of its former glory. The other consortium members breathed a sigh of relief. The VoR traffic numbers fell way behind those of the Welsh narrow gauge lines they really loved. BR had no intention of spending the large sums of money that would be needed if the line's capacity was to be exploited to the full. It turned to an arrangement whereby trains were run up the single line, now with no passing loops, in batches which even used all three locomotives simultaneously in high season if necessary. But the locomotive boilers were rebuilt at Swindon works and the carriages were also refurbished, on the platforms at Shrewsbury station where repair capacity happened to be available.

After the 1976 season, during which BR had to contribute to the costs of patrolling the forestry areas adjacent to the line to monitor and eliminate the risk of fire, investigation was made into the possibility of oil firing the steam locomotives. Collaborating with the Festiniog Railway, who had successfully achieved this objective on their line, No. 7 was equipped to burn oil during the winter of 1977-78, which led to all three locomotives being converted in turn. At Devil's Bridge, a port-a-cabin was installed in 1978 and

No. 9 *Prince of Wales* stands at Aberystwyth station on Saturday 13th April 1968, with the first public passenger train in BR rail blue livery which was chartered by the Stephenson Locomotive Society. The picture shows several of their members smartly dressed in sports jackets and wearing ties! Arthur Camwell, Secretary to the Midland Area of the SLS, organised the train, a departure from his normal specials which were usually to charter the last of the class or run the last train somewhere. Your author was on a family holiday in Wales as usual over that Easter weekend and cheekily asked 'Cam' if he could travel and was presented with a free ticket! The VoR train had to be seen for the first time in blue. No. 9 wears the then new double arrow symbol which was only ever applied to three British Railways steam locomotives – those on the Vale of Rheidol. Interestingly, the locomotive nameplate now has a red background, recalling the same colour as applied to those GWR steam locomotives repainted black after Nationalisation.

No. 9 *Prince of Wales* running round the same train on arrival at Devil's Bridge, the upper terminus of the railway, on 13th April 1968.

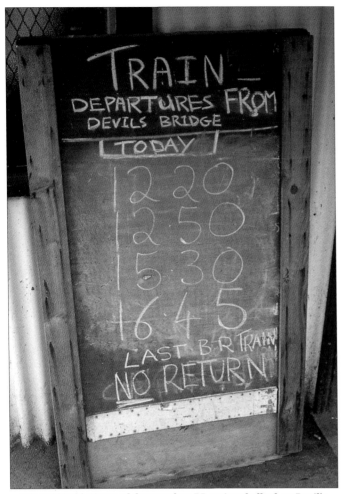

'NO RETURN'. Times of the very last BR trains chalked on Devil's Bridge noticeboard, on 18th December 1988.

Traveller's Fare ran a buffet, shop and waiting room in it. Thought had been given to sending a redundant 'Brighton Belle' Pullman car to Devil's bridge but the costs and logistics of transporting it there caused second thoughts.

From the 1980s, gala days were introduced which even saw named trains such as 'The Welsh Dragon' and the introduction of historical liveries with No. 8 *Llywelyn* being repainted into GWR green and, subsequently, No. 9 *Prince of Wales* being repainted into something like the original livery of yellow ochre carried at the line's opening. In 1986, *Mountaineer* visited from the Ffestiniog Railway, reviving an old 'tradition' of the FR lending locomotives in times of need as their England 0-4-0TT *Palmerston* had visited several times between the wars. Despite the various BR managers doing their level best to improve the Rheidol services imaginatively and with little extra money, the Vale of Rheidol's passenger figures were not good when compared with the other narrow gauge railways in the 'Great Little Trains of Wales' marketing group.

A derailment in 1986 led to questions being asked in Parliament about why British Rail was spending time operating a minor tourist railway when it should be concentrating on running a transport system. Shortly, privatisation would be back on the agenda. In 1988, BR finally announced that they would sell the $11^3/_4$ mile line, together with its three steam locomotives, the last operating under BR, and sixteen carriages and assorted wagons. Merchant bankers Lazard Brothers were retained to handle the sale process. The last BR steam trains would turn out to be an enthusiasts' day on 5th November and two Santa weekends over 10th-11th and 17th-18th December 1988. A group of local BR staff had announced their intention to

No. 8 *Llywelyn* , in unlined blue, crosses the Rheidol River viaduct.

make a bid to buy but were beaten in their objective by a commercial consortium of Tony Hills and Peter Rampton, co-owners of the Brecon Mountain Railway, to whom BR sold the Rheidol. There was much negotiation about the state of the Rheidol River bridge and other matters, legal issues to overcome concerning the transfer arrangements and considerable grumbling representations from the proposed management buy out but, eventually, by 29th March 1989, the British Railways Board (Vale of Rheidol) Light Railway (Amendment) Order was made and the line passed out of BR hands at last.

Whilst it was thus certain that steam trains would continue to run up the Rheidol Valley, and so the closure and transfer passed relatively unnoticed, there was an understandable air of sadness at Aberystwyth, BR's very last depot where working steam was a permanent feature of the roster. Several of the depot crew loved steam and had arranged transfers to Aberystwyth specifically to be able to work on the VoR. Not only was their 'management buy out' bid not accepted but several improvement suggestions they had made in the years running up to the transfer had not been implemented either: reinstatement of the Aberffrwd Loop, a local operating agreement for a nine hour day to increase flexibility and better advertising. These improvements would be left to the new private enterprise to implement which, to be fair, they have certainly done and more.

Driver Micky Richards and Fireman Jim Teague booked on No. 7 *Owain Glyndŵr* for the last day of BR's operation on Saturday 17th December. Just four people rode the morning train. The afternoon train fared better, running around half full. For them and their colleagues, the line had been 'Sold down the Rheidol.'

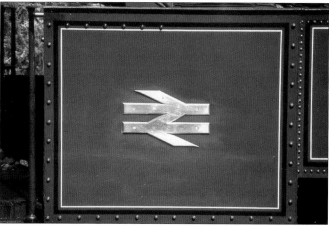

Brass BR double arrow logo adorning No. 7's black and white lined cabside.

No. 7 *Owain Glyndŵr* carries the slogan 'Sold down the Rheidol' on its smokebox on 18th December 1988, chalked up by the dispirited locomotive crew who had failed in their bid to secure a management buy-out of the line from British Rail.

On Monday 20th May 1968, No. 9 *Prince of Wales* with the first train to run from the new platforms at Aberystwyth station, formerly used by standard gauge trains to Carmarthen. [PBW]

On Easter Monday, 7th April 1969, No. 7 *Owain Glyndŵr* takes water from a standard gauge GWR water crane outside the former main line locomotive depot at Aberystwyth, to which all the locomotives and carriages were transferred as part of the George Dow plan, allowing the land formerly used by the narrow gauge for its station and depot to be sold.

No. 9 *Prince of Wales* blasts through the rock cutting immediately before Devil's Bridge in May, 1971. [PBW]

No. 9 *Prince of Wales* passing Blaendolau playing fields with the Cambrian line to Shrewsbury in the background. Llanbadarn station building and signal box can be seen in the left of the picture beyond the level crossing and the church of St. Padarn, the largest medieval church in mid Wales, to the right through the smoke. [PBW]

On 13th April 1968, No. 9 *Prince of Wales* takes water at Devil's Bridge in the cutting just below the station.

No. 7 *Owain Glyndŵr* prepares to leave Aberystwyth from the former Carmarthen line platforms with an Easter train on 7th April 1969.

In May 1971, No. 9 *Prince of Wales* runs along the shelf cut into the hillside to accommodate the railway, showing the scenic view of the Rheidol Valley and reservoir behind. [PBW]

No. 9 *Prince of Wales* rounds the 'S' bends near Devil's Bridge in May 1971. [PBW]

[ABOVE] No. 7 Ready to depart Devil's Bridge for the return downhill run. *Owain Glyndŵr* is now painted in a very smart fully lined out BR blue livery, red painted background to plates and brass double arrow logo.

[RIGHT] No. 7's nameplate.

[BELOW] No. 9 *Prince of Wales* stands on Aberystwyth ex-GWR locomotive depot in May 1982, repainted in a semblance of the railway's original livery, yellow ochre, by the order of David McIntosh, then the BR manager responsible for the line, based in Birmingham at Regional Railways.

[ABOVE] Llanbadarn station, forlorn and unloved in May 1978 but still open and featuring a GWR station bench seat.

[BELOW] Capel Bangor station, reduced to a single line request halt but still with black painted corrugated iron passenger waiting shelter, in May 1978.

In May 1971, No. 9 *Prince of Wales* crosses the wooden Rheidol River bridge, the subject of much price negotiation at the time of the purchase of the line by the Brecon Mountain Railway who were concerned at its condition. In modern times, the bridge has been completely rebuilt and this open view is no longer available due to a pedestrian bridge having been built alongside. [PBW]

One of the most important steam locomotives in any collection anywhere, shown on view in the National Trust's Penrhyn Castle Museum.

TEDDY BOSTON AND OTHER STORIES

10
TEDDY BOSTON
AND OTHER STORIES

Teddy Boston's Bagnall 0-4-0ST *Pixie* charges into the dark, round the 200 yards of track at the Cadeby Rectory on 5th November 1966. This image probably says it all about private narrow gauge railways at home, just from the faces of all the people on the train! An unusual shot from Ken Cooper's camera and the only one in his collection taken at night; he must have been truly inspired by the Almighty! [KC]

In the early 1950s, there were still literally hundreds of narrow gauge railways working for a living in the British Isles. As well as those which have since become preserved as heritage lines or bequeathed locomotives to them, many still served a multitude of industries but gradually ceased their usefulness and closed. Whilst the railway press gave most column inches to the decline of steam and the closure of lines on the national railway system, a growing band of enthusiasts energetically sought out narrow gauge railways and their industries, visiting slate quarries, brick works, steel mills, clay pits and many factories to record the dying embers.

The Welsh Highland Railway had given up the ghost in 1946 and much of its equipment was scrapped to help the war effort. But one steam locomotive escaped. *Russell*, a Hunslet 2-6-2T was bought by the Hook Norton Ironstone Railway in Oxfordshire and subsequently moved to the Fayle & Co. tramway at Purbeck in Dorset, running there as an 0-6-2T with the front pony truck removed to try to prevent derailments on the lightly laid track. The final straw was when *Russell's* driving axle sheared and so it was withdrawn. About that time, the Birmingham Locomotive Club was negotiating to buy *Secundus*, one of the railway's original locomotives for preservation at the Birmingham Science Museum, as it was one of the very few built in Birmingham. The club were also offered *Russell* for its £70 scrap price and so bought it as well, subject to finding a suitable home. Caernarvon Town Council were not able to help and, as some of the BLC members were then becoming involved in reviving the Talyllyn Railway in Wales and also beginning to develop a small museum, *Russell* was delivered to Wharf station at Towyn, where it was repainted and put on display. Hunslets very generously repaired the broken axle. The Festiniog Railway enquired about the possibility of having the locomotive which would certainly have helped its locomotive crisis. But, the TR folk, who in all reality had control of *Russell*, probably wanted to keep the locomotive on display (after all it had only just arrived) and they were very

George Sholto at Bressingham in 1988, now in green livery and with a new boiler and firebox. Well known railway historian Rodney Weaver is in centre of the three people on the footplate.

possibly also wary of the locomotive being further butchered to make it fit the FR loading gauge (remember, it had been cut down before with this in mind but unsuccessfully as it got 'stuck' in Moelwyn Tunnel). So, whilst not turning down the request, they imposed draconian conditions that made it impractical. However, when proposals were made to re-open the WHR, it was more natural that *Russell* should move on, initially being stored in Shropshire before at last returning to Wales.

All this helped encourage the formation of the Narrow Gauge Railway Museum Trust, based at Towyn Wharf but independent from the Talyllyn Railway, which subsequently gained charitable status with initial trustees appointed by the railway, the Newcomen Society, the Stephenson Locomotive Society and the Railway Correspondence & Travel Society. This museum trust and the Talyllyn Railway volunteers were in a good position to set about collecting almost anything they could lay their hands on relating to the narrow gauge in the British Isles and they have now amassed an enviable collection of artefacts. The first locomotive to arrive was *George Henry*, a vertical boilered de Winton from the Penrhyn Railway, quickly followed by a squat 0-4-0T from the Guinness brewery in Dublin. A TRPS member simply wrote and asked Guinness for it and the firm said yes and, before the TR even knew anything about it, the locomotive was on its way! Exhibits were gathered very quickly. Beyer, Peacock gave their delightful works shunter, an 0-4-0WT named *Dot*, whilst a French Courpet Louvet 0-6-0T, *Cambrai*, arrived from the Northampton ironstone lines but had to live outside next to

the TR platform as it was too large to go in the refurbished museum. *Pet*, a rather top heavy and tiny 0-4-0ST, came from the L&NWR's internal 18ins gauge works system at Crewe, *Rough Pup* represented the ubiquitous 'Quarry Hunslet' type and *Jubilee 1897*, a Manning Wardle 0-6-0ST design unique to the Welsh quarry systems, also came from Penrhyn. The collection comprises much more than locomotives, including for example a fascinating 4ft gauge Padarn Railway transporter wagon, complete with its set of three wooden 2ft gauge slate wagons and guard's brake van.

Towyn was far from unique in setting the scene for narrow gauge railway preservation, although people from the Midlands were certainly the first. In Leeds, the Narrow Gauge Railway Society was formed with a wide remit to study such railways; members enjoyed many early visits to ride on and photograph the last rites of its mission. Ron Redman was one of its leading lights. He wanted a job at Hudswell Clarke & Co. Ltd, one of the foremost engine manufacturers based in Leeds. He simply turned up at the front door and was engaged immediately as an engineering apprentice due to his academic record. Billy Clayton, the Works Manager, told him *"young men like you are what this industry needs"* and presented him with a £5 note after his initial hard work! He joined the NGRS at its second meeting and subsequently held the posts of librarian, secretary, chairman and president. Ron arranged annual coach tours to railways of interest, nicknamed 'monsoon tours' because it nearly always rained. He was a diligent researcher and contributed to a number of publications, always happy to share his knowledge.

In April 1971, Bagnall's 0-4-0ST of 1919 *Pixie* stands ready for business at the only station on the Cadeby Light Railway, owned and run by Teddy Boston. The line ran in a crescent shape round the rectory garden and the ride was 'out and propel back', with no run round loops. On the occasion I was allowed to drive *Pixie* when a teenager, I shut the regulator several yards before the 'end of track', only to be mildly admonished by Teddy, who simply opened the regulator once more saying there were yards to go yet!

Most people would think of *Russell* as a Welsh engine and they would be right, for it is synonymous with the Welsh Highland Railway but it was built in England, by Hunslet in Leeds, and finished its working life in Dorset after a sojourn in Oxfordshire. If it was not for the Birmingham Locomotive Club being interested in purchasing another engine and picking *Russell* up along the way, it would have been scrapped. Here the engine sits in a coat of almost luminous green by the Narrow Gauge Railway Museum at Towyn, in theory on display on 22nd July 1961. [KC]

The TR obtained second-hand rails from some of the Northampton ironstone railways and, at the same time, the museum collected various nameplates and other ephemera from scrapped locomotives, together with a complete locomotive. *Cambrai* stands outside the museum at Towyn Wharf on 22nd July 1961, having arrived the year before. Also seen at work in the first of these albums, it was one of two French-built locomotives delivered to Northamptonshire, built by Courpet Louvet in 1888. It was presented by the owners of the mines, Stewarts & Lloyds, but received some criticism due to its large size requiring it to be displayed outside. [KC]

Harold Dalston, a TR volunteer, saw a new narrow gauge diesel locomotive destined for the Guinness brewery in Dublin on display at the Festival of Britain exhibition in 1951. Rightly deducing that Guinness would be replacing their steam locomotives with diesels, he wrote to the Chairman of the brewery and asked if one of their unusual steam locomotives could be saved for preservation. The Chairman not only presented a locomotive but delivered it to Wales free of charge. Here, the acquisition stands behind the gunpowder shed at Towyn Wharf on 28th September 1957. [KC]

Locomotive preservation was a cause dear to his heart and, in 1954, he became involved in securing *Peter*, a standard Bagnall 0-4-0ST design, followed by *Barber*, an 0-6-2ST from Thos. Green, *Jack*, a Hunslet 0-4-0WT and then *Lord Granby*, a Hudswell, Clarke 0-4-0ST in 1961, all organised by the NGRS on behalf of Leeds City Museums. Amongst other equipment, he even negotiated the repatriation of *Junin*, Hudswell, Clarke's pioneer diesel-hydraulic of 1930 which had managed to survive in Chile.

One of the significant achievements of the NGRS has been the establishment of its library which continues to grow in content and stature; it contains a huge amount of information about any narrow gauge railway anywhere you might care to mention. Moreover, material is available on loan to members just on payment of the return postage. It is one of the great narrow gauge archives of the world.

In Lincolnshire, a new narrow gauge line was built by a group of enthusiasts who wanted to preserve the stock and the atmosphere of the potato railways from the area. Land was leased from Grimsby Rural District Council and equipment collected from all manner of former enterprises: Nocton Estates' First World War Hudson bogie wagons used for potatoes, the coach from the Sand Hutton Light Railway and the last remaining two coaches from the Ashover Railway. A 6-coupled Peckett saddle tank, *Jurassic*, provided the motive power and the railway even provided a public service to the Fitties Holiday Camp; by 1964, the railway was carrying 60,000 people at weekends and bank holidays, although it had to give up weekday traffic to the Grimsby-Cleethorpes Transport bus service as it could not compete effectively with it. Sadly, officialdom defeated the enthusiasts when the local authority insisted on the line being enclosed by a 6ft high fence on both sides and, faced with several obstacles, the

railway closed but has since been revived on another site.

Bernard Latham was the Secretary to the Industrial Locomotive Society and found several locomotives and artefacts well worth keeping but with no home to go to. The solution was the National Trust's Penrhyn Castle, appropriate too as it was the former home of the Douglas-Pennant family, who owned Penrhyn Quarry and its narrow gauge railway at Bethesda in North Wales. The stable block, offered for use as a museum, had restricted access, which would limit it to industrial and narrow gauge types, but this had its advantage as the first occupants were from the Penrhyn Railway. *Charles*, one of the three 'main line' locomotives built by Hunslets in 1882, was taken out of service when its boiler was condemned in 1955 (although records show it making one last trip in 1958!). In 1960, it was planned to scrap the locomotive but Iorweth Jones, a quarry employee and driver, saw *Charles* in the yard and sought help from Mr Tetley, the National Trust's area agent, who lost no time in approaching Lady Janet Douglas Pennant. She agreed to *Charles* joining the Museum collection.

The Douglas-Pennant family were probably surprised to find the National Trust becoming interested in some other family treasures, apart from their home and its contents at the castle itself. This resulted in a home for the line's 4-wheeled saloon, a quarrymens' open coach and a slate wagon, together with one of the quarry Hunslet 0-4-0STs, *Hugh Napier*, as well as *Charles*.

The Dinorwic Quarry, quite remarkably, still had *Fire Queen*, one of its two original 4ft gauge tender locomotives and the Padarn Railway's 4-wheeled saloon carriage. When the Dinorwic Quarry 'main line' between the quarry and Port Dinorwic was reconstructed to carry more traffic, the gauge was simply doubled to 4ft. Although an unusual

One of the Penrhyn Railway's 'Large Quarry' Hunslet 0-4-0STs, *George Sholto*, at Bressingham repainted in blue livery on 28th August 1967. Alan Bloom purchased the locomotive in 1966 for £100, together with four of the open quarrymens' carriages and some rails to build the new Nursery Railway at Bressingham. [KC]

A close-up of *Fire Queen's* nameplate and cylinders.

gauge in the British Isles, it had local logic as the narrower 2ft slate wagons could simply be carried two abreast on transporter wagons on the wider gauge, which helped reduce transshipment breakages. Two steam locomotives were ordered from A. Horlock of North Fleet Iron Works in 1848, at a price of £1,500 each. Although not a specialist in railway locomotives, the works delivered *Jenny Lind* and *Fire Queen*, both built in accordance with T. R. Crampton's patent No. 11,760 of 1847 as 4-coupled tender locomotives. Unusually, they had no frames; all wheels and fittings were attached to the boiler by individual brackets. The locomotives had a very long wheelbase and were fitted with Stephenson's valve gear driven by eccentrics on the leading axle. *Fire Queen* was taken out of service for overhaul in 1886 and has never worked since as her boiler was found to be in worse condition than expected and, by that time, new Hunslet 0-6-0Ts had arrived to take over. But the locomotive was not scrapped as, so rumour goes, the owner's daughter had a fond spot for *Fire Queen* ensuring it was preserved in a building all to itself just across the way from the main Dinorwic workshops, now themselves a leading industrial museum. Amazingly, *Fire Queen* remained safe and secure for eighty-three years being regularly cleaned and greased. A quite remarkable survivor from a past age and one of the most important steam locomotives in any collection anywhere.

Bernard Latham also collected several locomotives himself and initially stored them and even ran them on a short piece of track in his garden at his home! These included *Triassic*, *William Finlay* and *Lilla*. This is what Bernard wrote about acquiring *Triassic*: '*It was in 1956 when acting in my capacity of Honorary Secretary of the Industrial Locomotive Society that I organised a visit to the Southam works of the Rugby Portland Cement Company Limited, and learned that their narrow gauge railway system was to be superceded by road transport in the following year. I began to consider whether I could accommodate one of their redundant locomotives on my site. At that time I had no idea how much such a project would cost, nor what other complications or considerations would arise in connection with placing a locomotive in the garden in the middle of a domestic area.*

Undaunted, on 30th January 1957 I made my first tentative enquiry to the Rugby Portland Cement Company, and they lost little time in agreeing to sell to me one of their locomotives on very reasonable terms. So far so good. My next move was to make up my mind which locomotive was the most attractive proposition, and not being an engineer I might as well have picked one out with a pin. I decided that Triassic *was the most suitable, partly because it had on its side a plate reading* 'Rebuilt 1951' *and partly because it looked to have been the last of the quartet in use.*'

Elsewhere, several other former Penrhyn Quarry Hunslet locomotives were acquired by individuals. In Norfolk, Alan Bloom created an estate railway on his plant nursery near Diss, together with fairground equipment, standard gauge and miniature railway locomotives. *Gwynedd* and *Edward Sholto* can still be seen running round in circles at weekends giving holiday makers rides but, sadly, no longer with Alan at the regulator, his long white hair flowing over his shoulders. In the early days of his railways, informality reigned as everything was on his private land and he had little need to consult the Railway Inspectorate. The Whitehouse family spent a happy weekend riding the trains and Alan invited us on the footplate of *Gwynedd*. After one circuit, Alan handed over the regulator to us simply saying "*enjoy yourselves, you*

Fletcher, Jennings & Co. Ltd of Whitehaven are well known for building *Talyllyn* and *Dolgoch* but the firm also built a range of other industrial engines. Here we see *Townsend Hook* on 24th May 1961 at Sheffield Park, the first engine to arrive at the embryo Bluebell Railway even before the famous LB&SCR 'Terrier' *Stepney*. *Townsend Hook* was built to the unusual gauge of 3ft 2¹/₄ins in 1880 for the Dorking Greystone Lime Co. and rescued by the London Area Group of the Narrow Gauge Railway Society. She is now being restored as a static exhibit not too far from her original preservation home, at the Amberley Museum & Heritage Centre in West Sussex. [KC]

The 0-4-0WT *Jack*, built by Hunslet in 1898 (Works No. 684) at John Knowles' Metal Box at Woodville on 20th September 1952. This lovely locomotive carried on working until 1957 and was then donated to the Leeds Industrial Museum. [KC]

know what to do." PBW and I spent the rest of the afternoon happily taking it in turns to drive and fire this venerable locomotive on the public trains without further ado, instruction or examination. Fortunately, she is a very simple locomotive to master and we learned quickly!

One *'jolly round man, much given to Anglo-Saxon language in times of stress"* was none other than the Rector of Cadeby and Vicar of Sutton Cheney in Leicestershire, Teddy Boston. In May 1962, Teddy bought a 2ft gauge Bagnall 0-4-0ST named *Pixie* and set about building a short railway for it to run on in the Rectory grounds, with the permission of the Bishop of course; it was all of two hundred yards but enthusiasts flocked to it, enjoying Teddy's generosity and marveling at his very extensive 00 gauge railway, on which he ran a significant number of Triang models that he brutally carved up to represent almost every type of GWR locomotive that railway ever ran.

Teddy was a close friend of Rev'd Wilbert Awdry, the creator of both 'Thomas the Tank Engine' and the 'Skarloey Railway', a kindred spirit with whom he shared many railway holidays, not least to the re-opening of the Isle of Man as we have already read about elsewhere in these pages. Wilbert Awdry wrote of Teddy that *'he was a Parish Priest first and a steam enthusiast second. He never forced religion on anyone; but his sincere faith and devotion was there for all to see. Our family went to one of Teddy Boston's steam rallies and, after a jolly afternoon during which Teddy let us both drive his favourite* Pixie *and operate his OO railway trains, he exhorted us and the crowd to join him for Evensong and asked PBW to take the collection. Not being able to find the silver salver for the collection, Teddy grabbed a flower vase, tipped the flowers and water out of it and thrust it into PBW's hands. "Here, use this. God is more concerned that people give than what they put their gifts in...".*

The two Reverends are immortalised in *Duke the Lost Engine'*, when they stumbled across *Duke*, a Festiniog

Teddy Boston preaches from the footplate of his traction engine *Fiery Elias.*

England engine look alike on a carbon copy of the Corris Railway on the Island of Sodor. However, it was *Skarloey, Rheneas, Peter Sam* and the other little red engines the Rev'd Awdry invented for the narrow gauge, based entirely on true stories from the Talyllyn Railway, on which he was also a guard, which introduced a whole generation of railway preservation pioneers to their subject.

Lincolnshire Coast Light Railway shed and yard at Humberstone. [KC]

A train stands in North Sea Lane station on the Lincolnshire Coast Light Railway on 3rd September 1966. The blue and white coach is the most interesting and indeed only piece of rolling stock on the train. It was built by the Gloucester Railway Carriage & Wagon Company Ltd in 1924 for the Ashover Light Railway, which ran in the Derbyshire Peak District. The LCLR bought the remaining two coaches for £50 for its railway at Humberstone near Cleethorpes. [KC]

Another ex-Penrhyn Railway quarry locomotive, *Gwynedd*, at Bressingham repainted in blue livery and seen here working on the estate's Nursery Railway on 28th August 1967. *Gwynedd* was built in 1888 by Hunslets and is one of the 'Port' Class 0-6-0STs.

No. 7 *Tom Rolt* stands at Brynglas with three matching TR bogie carriages on 6th May 1991, immediately before running up to Abergynolwyn for its naming ceremony.

11
IRISH PETE: THE DEMOCRATIC LOCOMOTIVE

Irish Pete **stands in front of the gunpowder store at Wharf soon after arrival at Easter 1969.**

Board Na Mona (the Irish Turf Board) used a light railway with diesel locomotives to bring peat from the bogs to a turf burning electric power station at Clonsast, about fifty miles from Dublin. In an effort to save fuel and use turf instead, three Class 'E' 3ft gauge 0-4-0WT steam locomotives were ordered from Andrew Barclay, Sons & Co, Kilmarnock in 1948 but they were only used for a few years as the fuel proved unsuitable. Two were bought for preservation in Ireland and the Talyllyn Railway bought the third, Works No. 2263 which arrived at the railway on 26th March 1969, initially being stored at Wharf station. It was virtually an enlarged version of the railway's No. 6 *Douglas* from the same makers. The plan was to dismantle it and use the main components with a new frame to build a suitable sixth steam locomotive for the railway to power the heavier trains expected from increasing traffic.

Almost from the moment when it arrived, controversy reigned over what it should be called. A mischievous person chalked up *Irish Pete* on No. 2263, causing discussion to rage over many a pint in the Towyn hostelries. Of course, *Irish Pete* was a play on words reflecting the locomotive's antecedents.

The Talyllyn Railway Preservation Society always puts great store on democratic principles and so it was that the in-house journal editorial published before the AGM in 1970 exhorted members to come and vote for a name for the new No. 7, even before it had been rebuilt. Names for the other five steam locomotives had been simple to decide. *Talyllyn* and *Dolgoch* were already so named before the TRPS was ever thought of. The two Corris locomotives were aptly named *Sir Haydn* and *Edward Thomas* after the railway's previous owner and its faithful manager. *Douglas* was given to the railway by Douglas Ableson. So what to call No. 7? There was no shortage of ideas. Six names were selected by the railway's Council to be voted on by the membership: Earl of Northesk, Cader Idris, Tom Rolt, Meirion, James Swinton Spooner and Irish Pete.

At the Talyllyn Railway Preservation Society AGM held on 3rd October 1970, a vote was duly taken on the name which should be bestowed on the new No. 7. The winner was *Irish Pete*! The Hon. Secretary declared that the railway had not yet lost its sense of humour. Ninety-eight votes had been cast for *Irish Pete*, which won by a margin of just twenty-four votes, 250 votes having been cast. The Society had about

'Forward by steam'. Buffer beam headboard on No. 6 *Douglas*, fellow Andrew Barclay locomotive, to celebrate the naming of *Tom Rolt* on 6th May 1991.

Mike Green bolts the nameplate *Tom Rolt* onto No. 7 at Quarry Siding, immediately prior to the naming ceremony on 6th May 1991.

Tom Rolt unveiled. Sonia Rolt has pulled the Welsh flag from No. 7 to reveal the nameplate in public for the first time during the commissioning at Abergynolwyn station on 6th May 1991.

2,500 members. All proving the importance of turning up at a meeting to vote if you feel strongly about something. The AGM was properly convened.

All hell now broke loose and the in house magazine was to make interesting reading over the coming months and years, to say nothing of the local pub talk amongst volunteers:

'I am appalled at the irresponsibility of those who voted for this name, which is far too frivolous and inappropriate for an important locomotive on a very important narrow gauge railway.'

'I think all we can say after this ballot is that the majority of members oppose the name.'

'I consider that a graceful compliment should have been paid to Mr Rolt for his untiring and unstinting work for the railway in its early days.'

'How children will love Irish Pete. *It will give great scope for publicity, and I hope the Rev. Awdry will use his marvellous imagination and give the children another Talyllyn story.'*

But, for nearly twenty years, No. 7 slumbered in the south carriage shed at Pendre, its rebuild unfinished. Of course, when purchased in 1969, there was then no way of knowing that the railway was nearing the end of two decades of traffic growth, requiring longer and heavier trains. Furthermore, the deficiencies experienced with the two original locomotives since their rebuilding, especially with *Talyllyn*, had largely been rectified and both No's 1 and 2 were now capable of performing useful tasks. So there was no economic case for investing in a larger and more powerful locomotive the railway did not need.

However, during 1987, the boiler inspector sounded warnings about the condition of the boiler of No. 6 *Douglas* and so thoughts turned once again to finishing No. 7 and storing *Douglas* until funds could be raised for its new boiler. After all, No. 6 was now an historic locomotive in its own right and with an important Talyllyn pedigree.

Of course, no sooner had work restarted on converting the parts of No. 7 into becoming a useful locomotive than tongues began to wag once more about its chosen name. A fair argument was put forward that the locomotive had now spent most of its life in Wales and, even the time it spent in Ireland was largely in store having failed to convince Bord Na Mona that it could be a useful turf burner.

So, at the Society AGM on 4th June 1989, Council once again decided that the membership could vote on a name for No. 7. This time the choice was slightly wider: Cader Idris, Earl of Northesk, Heart of Gold, Irish Pete, Nant Gwernol, Prince William and Tom Rolt. Council also decided that transferable voting would be used, with members invited to put numbers against as many names as they wished in order of preference. *Tom Rolt* beat *Cader Idris* by just four

votes, gathering 129 votes in support. There were no more substantive complaints.

The well known Norwich shedmaster, Bill Harvey, who had helped out a little in the very early days, summed up the decision well once No. 7 had been rebuilt: *'I had the pleasure and privilege of sharing with Tom Rolt the excitement and vicissitudes of his 'Railway Adventure,' and assisting him in his*

Sonia and *Tom Rolt* stand proudly together after the nameplate unveiling at Abergynolwyn on 6th May, 1991.

efforts to maintain a daily passenger train service over what could then be described only as a charming but thoroughly run down ramshackle little slate railway. I am sure that Tom would be extremely proud of what has been achieved since those pioneering days. No. 7 must surely be ranked as John Bate's master work for the ingenuity he has displayed in the design and construction of a virtually new engine, and to quote him: "The TR has now moved into the 20th century!"'

Many designs had been suggested for a new locomotive for the Talyllyn, even at one stage enquiring from Hunslets if they would build another example of their small *Eva* 0-4-2T, which is likely to have been quite suitable but the price was then beyond the TR's reach. The ability to buy No. 2263 for roughly scrap price proved the solution. It was decided to do all the conversion work at Pendre, including making new frames and creating an 0-4-2T. The workshop facilities were upgraded to enable reconstruction which began in 1971 and, interspersed with the need to complete new carriages, work on the frames was well advanced by 1973. That year saw an all time record of 186,000 passenger journeys but then a fall in traffic made No. 7 redundant and all efforts turned to maintaining the existing fleet of locomotives and carriages until 1988, following the concern over No. 6's boiler.

Work recommenced and continued steadily until the decision to hold a naming ceremony on 6th May 1991 required some 'short cuts' to enable the locomotive to be at least steamed for the event, even if it could not be released into service straight away. The locomotive was

No. 7 *Tom Rolt* in service running round at Nant Gwernol station on 4th May 1992.

completed as a side tank, provided with a distinctive whistle of John Bate's choice, modelled on that used by the Australian Puffing Billy Railway, and a chimney modified from one purchased at the Dinorwic Quarry sale in 1971. By this time, it had been decided to equip all the locomotives and rolling stock with air brakes and so No. 7's design incorporated the necessary features from the start.

Sonia Rolt was asked to name the locomotive after her late husband and did so with panache at Brynglas station on 6th May 1991. After unveiling the nameplate, Sonia remarked during the naming that No. 7 might well be the newest locomotive on the railway but it had the oldest boiler! She then broke a bottle of champagne over No. 7's left front buffer and, as she did so, *Tom Rolt's* safety valves lifted.

After the naming ceremony, No. 7's first revenue earning trips were on a shuttle service to Hendy, topped and tailed with *Edward Thomas* on 27th July 1991 for the Tywyn Hospital charity show.

The last word goes to Dr Harold Vickers, one of the early

Sonia Rolt beside No. 7 *Tom Rolt* at Abergynolwyn on 6th May 1991, speaking about her husband preparatory to unveiling the nameplate.

volunteers: '*Our new loco* Tom Rolt *is a worthy memorial to a remarkable man and John Bate is to be congratulated on producing such an attractive machine, with clean functional lines, no gimmicks, and lots of character.*"

Rear three-quarter portrait of No. 7 *Tom Rolt* on the level crossing at Brynglas on 6th May 1991, immediately prior to its naming ceremony.

Joan belches out black smoke whilst she stands at Welshpool's Raven Square station in September 1985, as the fireman builds up her fire ready for the ascent on Golfa Bank from a standing start. *Joan* was built in 1927 by Kerr, Stuart & Co. Ltd (Works No. 4404) and exported to the Antigua Sugar Company in the West Indies. She is of the maker's standard 'Martary' Class and features a balloon style chimney as a spark arresting device. Originally painted green in sugar line service, she entered W&LLR traffic in smart Midland red.

12
LIGHT RAILWAY RENAISSANCE FROM WELSHPOOL

The Earl at Welshpool's Smithfield yard with the Chairman's re-opening train to Llanfair on Saturday 6th April 1963. The two carriages were both from the Admiralty's Lodge Hill & Upnor Railway. The first is a standard toastrack seating up to forty passengers in five doorless compartments (with your author in his school uniform standing in the doorway to the first compartment) and the second is the Combination Car, a First/Second/Guard's carriage, formerly used to convey officers and NCOs in either a compartment for six or a saloon for fourteen people. Both the carriages have been sold on, the toastracks to the Sittingbourne & Kemsley Railway and the Combination Car to the new Welsh Highland Railway, where it is now downgraded for use by permanent way staff. For the 1963 re-opening of the W&LLR, it proudly carried the Society's Chairman and the current Earl of Powis. [PBW]

Nowadays, the Welsh coast can be reached from the Midlands in under three hours by car by driving through the beautiful and undulating Welsh Marches countryside populated by various castles and fortified manor houses from the Middle Ages. To some extent, the region is largely unchanged and still has many small farms and black & white timbered cottages. One hundred and fifty years ago, the Welsh Marches were very remote and, even with the advent of the standard gauge railways, only the key market towns were connected to the network. This led several of the smaller towns to seek to build feeder lines to enable villagers and produce to access markets but it was hard to raise the capital finance. So, in 1896, Government passed the Light Railways Act to help relieve this burden and make it easier for communities to build their own railways. Several were built to various narrow gauges as this was cheaper still. Lines could simply follow the contours of the land and adjacent roadways. The

Welshpool & Llanfair Light Railway (W&LLR) was just one of these, built to connect the small town of Llanfair Caereinion, nestling in the hills, to the larger market town of Welshpool and permit transfers to the Cambrian Railways, providing access to Shrewsbury and further afield in England. As Ralph Cartwright succinctly put it in his classic history of the line: '*use of the narrow gauge, tangling with the town and piercing the hill country with grinding curves and capricious gradients, truly tapped the Act's same spirit of purpose.*'.

The railway is an excellent and rare example of a 19th century solution to a problem of considerable interest even in modern times: that of providing a cost effective public transport solution in thinly populated rural areas on the verge of extinction due to lack of jobs and the continuing local emigration to cities. The Welshpool & Llanfair Light Railway Preservation Company Limited has brought this little line back to life but now for tourists. Whilst the shrill shriek of its steam locomotives' whistles echo and re-echo

On 1st October 1961, before the formal re-introduction of passenger services, *The Earl* stands at Castle Caereinion with a train of two Upnor toastrack carriages and an original W&LLR brakevan. In the background one of the original W&LLR cattle vans can also be seen. [ESR]

across the Powys hills, its story and significance and also that of its gauge, local and now international connections, perhaps still remain to be shouted from the rooftops as history repeats itself, and more and more connections are made with Britain's colonial past.

This little line, nearly ten miles long, was built to the 2ft 6ins gauge, which was to prove a most fortuitous gauge when it came to be preserved. Quite by co-incidence, very many British Colonial and also European lines, built for similar purposes, were constructed to the same gauge and so could bequeath rolling stock sorely needed by the Preservation Society to expand its tourist services in the modern era. Beyer, Peacock & Co. Ltd, locomotive builders to the world, were contracted to produce two, twin sturdy 0-6-0Ts which were appropriately named *The Earl* and *The Countess*, after the residents of Powis Castle, which is connected with Clive of India, the founder of the famous East India Company which established a firm pattern for British colonialisation and Commonwealth. These two locomotives faithfully hauled all the market traffic and its passengers up the sinewy line beside the Banwy River all its working life. The Welshpool & Llanfair Railway survived to be Nationalised and it carried on manfully until 1956, bringing mainly coal traffic to Llanfair. Fortunately, it survived into the post-Second World War years when voluntary railway preservation schemes emerged which were to save its life but only just in time and not without considerable effort.

The first voluntary railway preservation schemes were also in Wales and also narrow gauge: the Talyllyn Railway and the Ffestiniog Railway. Both were owned by statutory

companies and had not been Nationalised and so their shareholdings could, with luck, good connections and endeavour, be bought or given away. Not so, the Welshpool & Llanfair, which was now a Nationalised concern and any dealings by volunteers had to be with the British Transport Commission. Fortunately, they were somewhat sympathetic. Various rescue attempts and schemes were discussed even before the line closed to traffic but it took a London printer by the name of William Morris to get the ball rolling. He organised a special train over the line on 15th September 1956, attracting seventy enthusiasts who had an exhilarating ride in the open goods wagons. Several joined a new society proposed by Morris to save the railway. This was true pioneering as it was the first serious attempt to rescue a state owned railway, presenting some formidable financial and legal problems which had never been encountered before. A public meeting was held in the Fred Tallant Hall, near Euston, a venue which became dear to the heart of railway enthusiasts with a particular interest in overseas railways and where the famous Continental Railway Circle held its monthly meetings for many a year.

There was good and bad news. British Railways were willing to sell. But Welshpool Town Council had changed their tune and were now vehemently against the railway being reopened through the town section as they wanted to redevelop the cattle market area and build a town road by-pass. Oliver Veltom, Area Manager, Oswestry, had arranged for both *The Earl* and *The Countess* to be squirreled away in safekeeping at Oswestry works and a solicitor, Stanley Keyse, was prepared to put his shoulder to the wheel to work out

The re-opening train hauled by *The Earl* approaches Raven Square and the beginning of the section of the railway that was transferred to the Preservation Society. [ESR]

a solution for an appropriate structure to save the railway: to safeguard the individual interests of volunteers, leading to the formation of the Preservation Society as a company limited by guarantee with each member having only one vote and so preventing any one or more individuals from gaining control. Whilst this secured the democratic objective and also provided a body corporate able to negotiate and conclude a purchase agreement with British Rail, it did not by itself solve the fundraising need.

However, British Railways were, rather surprisingly perhaps, prepared to agree a lease purchase on terms which were within the reach of the nascent society. In 1959, terms were provisionally agreed for a forty-two year lease, with the locomotives and rolling stock to be paid for by hire purchase over ten years, subject to Ministry of Transport approval to carry passengers for the first time since 7th February 1931. Track and lineside clearance began with volunteer working parties. A selection of which wagons to keep was made and these were removed from the town sidings by a couple of carthorses borrowed by the Society, newly shod for the occasion and with volunteers pushing the wagons from behind. The original two steam locomotives were returned from Oswestry after some repairs and soon their sounds were heard once again climbing the steep Golfa Bank out of Welshpool, largely enabled by the generosity of John Wilkins, a Midlands washing machine entrepreneur who had earlier saved the Fairbourne Railway and made it his own and also been a key benefactor to the Talyllyn. First, *The Earl* returned after some minor repairs, to be followed by *The Countess* after rather more substantial work. When

The Countess finally arrived on a 'Flatrol' wagon in a pick-up goods train and was shunted overnight to the cattle dock for an overnight layover, *The Earl* was lit up at Llanfair and made the special journey down the line to Welshpool to 'meet the wife'. The two locomotives double-headed back to Llanfair up Golfa Bank, perhaps the first time in history there had ever been a double-header as there would have been no such need in ordinary every day service.

On 3rd October 1962, the British Transport Commission (Welshpool & Llanfair) Light Railway (Leasing & Transfer Order) was made, effective from 12th October, which transferred the railway to the Preservation Society but excluding the section from Welshpool town to Raven Square on the outskirts. At last, the Preservation Society had the control it wanted. Now it needed some carriages as all three originals had been scrapped in the 1930s. Luckily, the Society had chosen its Chairman wisely in Lt Col. Sir Thomas Salt as, through his good offices, the Admiralty were happy to make available a diesel locomotive and some carriages from its Lodge Hill & Upnor Railway by the Medway, which had only closed the year before and fortuitously was the same gauge. Preparations could now be made for the railway to re-open to the public and carry passengers.

On Saturday 6th April 1963, exactly sixty years to the day after the original opening ceremony, passenger trains ran from the Welshpool yard. Ironically, only the week before, British Railways had published the infamous Beeching Report recommending the drastic pruning of the nations' railway network.

At 11 o'clock, *The Earl* left Welshpool with Sir Thomas

The Earl crosses Raven Square with the Chairman's re-opening special. Your author peers out of the first compartment in the leading Admiralty carriage (fancy wearing school uniform at a weekend nowadays!), whilst PBW walks back to his car to continue the chase wearing his trusty 'Rollieflex' $2^1/_4$ins square format camera round his neck, with which all his post war black & white photographs were taken. [ESR]

The Earl pauses at Castle Caereinion with the inaugural re-opening train. This time, it is Thelma Whitehouse's turn to peer out from the Admiralty carriage. [ESR]

Salt's party, including the Earl of Powis, running to Llanfair Caereinion where Sir Thomas stood on a wagon and addressed the crowd: *"They say that history repeats itself. This is the diamond jubilee of the hour of the opening of the line sixty years ago by the then Earl of Powis."*. The current Earl was invited to re-open the railway and did so with the following words: *"It is a very great honour and pleasure for me to be invited because my family were intimately involved with the railway ... the first sod was cut by my cousin, Lord Clive, in 1901 and he was presented with this spade as a memento of the event. I am sure you would be wishing to join with me to congratulate the members of the Welshpool & Llanfair Light Railway on the great project which they have now brought to fruition ... they have got this railway back again through their very great efforts ... I have much pleasure in declaring this line open and asking you to join me in wishing it every prosperity and continued life hereafter."*.

The Earl then walked up to *The Countess* and drove her through a tape across the tracks to celebrate the re-opening. Following which, history repeated itself once again, as *The Countess* then returned the official party for a rather late lunch at the Royal Oak hotel in Welshpool. Meanwhile, *The Earl* left Llanfair at 1.30pm with the first public train running to Castle Caereinion and back. The use of the Welshpool town section was shortlived as the council had completed their purchase of the section and so a very last train was run, double-headed by both steam locomotives, on 17th August, 1963.

A new headquarters of the railway had to be established at Llanfair and, gradually, the Society got the yard there re-organised and was able to take over the coal yard to provide space to add much needed buildings for a workshop and locomotive shed. To start with, services were run only as far as Castle Caereinion. However, in 1964, operations were extended to Sylfaen, a halt near the top of the famous and very steep Golfa Bank, which the Railway Inspectorate was unwilling to allow the railway to use until continuous brakes had been fitted to the trains. Sadly, towards the end of 1964 heavy rains swelled the Banwy River and severely damaged the piers of the railway bridge over the river at Heniarth, resulting in its girders leaning drunkenly over the swirling current. Sir Thomas came to the rescue once again with his connections and arranged for the Army to effect repairs and enough money was raised by a national appeal so permanent disaster was averted but, sadly, Sir Thomas died the very next day after the former Admiralty diesel, *Upnor Castle*, crossed the repaired bridge with a test train.

More locomotives and rolling stock began to arrive which were much needed as, in reality, the Chattenden & Upnor carriages were not altogether suitable with open doorways and very restricted viewing from their hard wooden seats, as the carriages had no separate windows; it was also decided that they were not suitable for vacuum brakes which were a necessity if services were once again to run to Welshpool. One of the Society directors was Derek Mayman, who had forged links with the Zillertalbahn in Austria. He was a very kind and

The Countess, in unauthentic but attractive lined Cambrian Railways passenger livery, stands in Smithfield yard in the afternoon of 6th April 1963, with the first public train to carry passengers in the preservation era from Welshpool.[PBW]

Monarch stands at Llanfair Caereinion. Built by W.G. Bagnall in 1953 (Works No. 3024), this was the last steam locomotive to be built for ordinary commercial service in the British Isles. Bagnalls had introduced this design for sugar estate work in Natal, South Africa and suggested to Bowaters Lloyd Pulp & Paper Mills in Sittingbourne Kent that the double bogie Meyer design offered an advantage in weight distribution over that railway's viaduct. Painted in the Bowaters standard livery of medium green lined red, with black frames and brass nameplates, the name *Monarch* commemorated the Coronation of Queen Elizabeth II in the year the locomotive was built – 1953. *Monarch* arrived on the W&LLR in 1966 but was never a wholehearted success. After a misadventure on the Ffestiniog Railway, where she was to be rebuilt for use on the Welsh Highland Railway (or at least as proposed by two of their members), she has been returned to static display at Welshpool, now sporting a stovepipe chimney. [KC]

On 9th September 1962, *The Earl* stands at Llanfair Caereinion, resplendent in Great Western lined passenger locomotive livery. Whilst W&LLR engines were painted in GWR green they were never lined out; nevertheless, the livery suits No. 1 well. Note that the cab lining, which was being applied by the photographer, Ken Cooper, was as yet incomplete. The locomotive is one of two identical twins supplied by Beyer, Peacock & Co. Ltd in 1902 (Works No. 3496), renumbered 822 by the GWR. [KC]

On 2nd July 1966, *The Countess* stands at Llanfair Caereinion, in Cambrian Railways lined passenger locomotive livery, never carried by W&LLR engines in their heyday. This the other original Beyer, Peacock twin (Works No. 3497), renumbered 823 by the GWR. [KC]

On 12th June 1965, *Nutty* stands on the 'main line' at Llanfair Caereinion. Built by the Sentinel Waggon Works of Shrewsbury in 1929 (Works No. 7701) for the London Brick Company's 2ft 11ins gauge line in Huntingdonshire, specially to work within their 6ft loading gauge. When withdrawn, she was preserved by the Tywyn-based Narrow Gauge Railway Museum Trust, regauged to 2ft 6ins and brought to the railway in 1964-65, still in the original bright yellow livery. Her features included a vertical boiler, chain drive and twin cylinders, the latter mounted horizontally to keep within the required restricted height clearance. She was used primarily for maintenance trains but also on occasional passenger trains to Heniarth during the reconstruction of the Banwy River bridge. Whilst a reliable engine, she was hardly suitable for the railway, especially having a very cramped cab with the water gauge glasses being within a few inches of fireman's face. Rarely used after 1966, she left the railway in 1971 and can now be seen on static display at Stonehenge on the Leighton Buzzard Light Railway. [KC]

On 6th October 1962, *Upnor Castle* stands on the siding at Castle Caerinion in original Lodge Hill & Upnor Railway condition and dark green livery, lined in white. Built by F.C. Hibberd in 1954 (Works No. 3687) as one of their 'Planet' range, she arrived on the W&LLR in 1962, being named *Upnor Castle* on 22nd August, the name having been suggested by the Admiralty. The diesel was most useful but her short wheelbase led to rough riding. In 1968, the opportunity arose to purchase an 0-6-0D also from the Admiralty and so, in 1968, *Upnor Castle* was sold to the Ffestiniog Railway, where she was regauged to 1ft 11^1/$_2$ins and her wheelbase lengthened. The Ffestiniog then began a naming convention for their future diesels to follow the 'Castle' style when they acquired their second 'Planet" and subsequent diesels. [KC]

On 7th October 1962, *The Earl* approaches Llanfair Caereinion station with a train of three Admiralty carriages, the Combination Car being on the end and an original W&LLR brake van immediately behind the locomotive. [KC]

persuasive man and effected the transfer of four wooden-balconied carriages, which were surplus to requirements in Austria, to augment the W&L fleet. Incidentally, he also left no stone unturned to ensure the suburban line he used to commute to work, the famous North Warwickshire Line from Birmingham to Stratford upon Avon, was not closed as British Railways intended. These carriages, together with an 0-6-0 diesel, *Chattenden*, also from the Admiralty railway, and an unusual Meyer 0-4-4-0T *Monarch*, from Bowaters Paper Railway in Sittingbourne, were secured to augment the fleet. The W&LLR were indeed lucky that there were two 2ft 6ins gauge industrial lines which had survived long enough to provide stock and also that the 'standard' gauge of Eastern Europe's many narrow gauge lines was 760mm, as near as made no difference to 2ft 6ins. As reliance on the two Beyer, Peacock steam locomotives was thought insufficient in the long term (and as *Monarch* turned out to be less than ideal for the W&LLR's 'switchback' line) a further steam locomotive was sourced, also from Austria from the Steiermarkische Landesbahnen. This was an 0-8-0T built by Societe Franco-Belge in 1944 for the German military authorities in the Second World War but which fell into the hands of the American Occupation Forces at the end of hostilities. As one set of driving wheels is flangeless, it is able to negotiate the sharp curves of the W&LLR with ease and so was put into service quickly, named *Sir Drefaldwyn* (Welsh for the County of Montgomery in which the line runs) and in its Steiermark livery of black lined in red. Although initially somewhat controversial to import and use a Continental locomotive, the choice proved sound as the 0-8-0T was of modern construction and easily capable of hauling heavy trains as required

In time, further acquisitions were made. Member Tony Thorndike was on holiday in Antigua in the West Indies and spotted the Kerr, Stuart 0-6-2T *Joan* on that island's sugar railway network, which was now out of use but also to the 2ft 6ins gauge. He duly arranged for it to be repatriated. Not content with that, a visit was made to Sierra Leone in West Africa on closure of that country's 2ft 6ins railway system and, as a result, the W&LLR acquired four modern bogie carriages and a delightful Hunslet 2-6-2T ordered for the system by the Crown Colonies in 1954.

Two other steam locomotives must be mentioned, each at opposite ends of the spectrum in size. First, *Nutty*, a Sentinel vertical-boilered locomotive built for the London Brick Company and preserved by the Narrow Gauge Railway Museum Trust. Originally 1ft 11ins gauge, it was regauged for use on the W&LLR in 1964, painted in bright yellow livery, and proved somewhat useful in shunting and maintenance traffic but not in passenger service. Second, *Orion*, an enormous (for the W&LLR) 2-6-2T built in 1947 by Tubize in Belgium for the Finnish Jokioisten Railway. Whilst both had their promoters on the railway, neither were well suited and both have now left the line. The Sentinel is currently on display at the Leighton Buzzard Railway, whilst *Orion* has now been repatriated to Jokioisten and sees regular service there. *Monarch*, probably the third of a trio of unsuitable locomotives, also left the railway for a misadventure on the Ffestiniog Railway (where it was to be regauged and run

Mixed gauge at the cattle dock, all that remained of the goods transshipment facilities in Smithfield yard, Welshpool.

on the Welsh Highland) but has now returned and been reassembled for display at Welshpool.

Quite understandably, the W&LLR wanted to return trains to Welshpool, even though they would only be able to go as far as Raven Square. With much effort, two and a half miles of railway were eventually rebuilt and a new station constructed on land acquired next to the Raven Inn and road roundabout. After some misgivings, this transpired to be a satisfactory arrangement as the location was highly visible to all passing traffic. A redundant wooden station building was rescued from Eardisley and reconstructed. *Sir Drefaldwyn* arrived with the first train on 18th July 1981 and once again a formal recommissioning ceremony, was performed by the Earl of Powis, on 16th May, 1982. The Welshpool & Llanfair Light Railway was now complete. The trick for the railway's commercial department was now to get the cars to stop over on their way to the Welsh coast and, as roads improved, to promote day trips especially from the Midlands and North West.

The Countess bowls into Heniarth with a train of Admiralty carriages and a box van. Note the children (with dog!) leaning out of the carriage open doorways. Safety considerations led to some of these toastrack carriages being reconstructed with doors and windows before being sold on to the Sittingbourne & Kemsley Railway when the Zillertalbahn carriages arrived.

The view from Llanfair Caereinion station looking east on 19th September 1964, with the ground frame in place to work the points and former GWR signals before the signal box was built. [KC]

On 20th September 1964, *The Earl* heads a permanent way train at Cyfronedd with an original W&LLR brake van and then a coal wagon behind the locomotive, followed by an Admiralty low-sided bogie wagon.

In April 1968, *The Earl*, resplendent in lined GWR green, waits at Castle Caereinion with a Ffestiniog Railway Society special train of five Admiralty bogie carriages; a heavier train than would be permitted today, with the steep Golfa Bank now open for traffic. The carriages have all been repainted in a new red and white livery and the first two toastracks have been rebuilt with windows and doors.

The Countess at Castle Caereinion with a train of Admiralty carriages and a van. Note the middle former toastrack carriage has been reconstructed with windows and doors, whilst the station remains in original condition with its signal box.

On 26th March 1964, *The Earl* poses on Cyfronedd Viaduct with a ballast permanent way train. This train was run on a whim specially by Michael Polglaze, General Manager, for PBW (and CMW!) so they could get this picture and have a cab ride. Sadly, heavy tree growth now obscure this lovely view. [PBW]

Chattenden, the Admiralty 0-6-0D, stands at Llanfair Caereinion with a range of Lodge Hill Railway stock. This diesel locomotive was built by E.E. Baguley in 1949 to the order of the Drewry Car Company and carries Drewry's serial No. 2263. It was delivered new to the Admiralty Lodge Hill & Upnor Railway. When the Upnor line closed, the diesel was transferred to Ernsettle depot in Devon and then to Broughton Moor in Cumberland, being declared surplus in 1968 and purchased by the W&LLR, who had had their eyes on it for a long time. It is a most useful machine, capable of hauling a five coach passenger train as well as being suitable for shunting.

On 12th May 1973, the W&LLR ran a members' special train down Golfa Bank to Raven Square to celebrate the tenth anniversary of the railway's re-opening and make a statement about the intent to introduce regular services on this section. A contractor was hired to cut back some of the undergrowth and makeshift repairs were made to the track to enable the train to run. *The Earl*, with its three coaches, marked the successful descent of Golfa Bank by considerable whistling, reaching Raven Square at 12.25pm to be welcomed by the Mayor of Welshpool. Here the train is seen re-assembled for the return trip, which was one of three worked over the weekend.

The Countess crosses the Banwy River bridge with a train for Castle Caereinion. The first carriage behind the locomotive is the Admiralty Combination Car. The centre of the car side features the badge of the Royal Naval Armament Supply Department, with 'Upnor-Lodge Hill Railway' underneath it. The car contrasted with the spartan toastracks by having an all steel, flush-paneled body, full length doors, sliding windows and upholstered seats in the small compartment. The passenger facilities comprised the compartment for six and a saloon for fourteen people. Initially a supplement of 1s was charged for each single journey.

The Countess bowls along the grass grown track towards the Banwy bridge and Heniarth. These days children are discouraged from leaning out of carriage windows, let alone standing in the open doorways.

On 15th September 1985, the then Birmingham Railway Museum chartered the former Sierra Leone 2-6-2T and a special train as a thank you to its staff and volunteers for their hard work throughout the 150th anniversary celebrations for the GWR. Here, No. 85 is seen with the special at a photo-stop at the top of Golfa Bank on the return journey, hauling Zillertalbahn stock. No. 85 was the last of thirty-two similar locomotives built for the SLR by Hunslet as late as 1954 (Works No. 3815). The locomotive is shown here in the SLR mid green livery, worn in the years before the Second World War, after which they were turned out in black.

They came home with not one but two Irish narrow gauge steam locomotives and this is the tale of the jaunt which set the wheels in motion. We need to go back a bit before the opening years of this book but, no matter, it will be worth it. Let Edgar T. Mead relate:

'My first glimpse of the Donegal three foot gauge railway in Ireland was at Stranorlar. That March 1959 morning when I presented myself to Bernard L. Curran, Manager, he indicated in his calm and patient manner that railroad operations might not last very long, perhaps only to the end of the year. It was as though a thunderbolt went through me. From what I had read and was now seeing, the Donegal Railway was the quintessential permanent narrow gauge system, a high class line with good track, dependable train service and, at least reasonable traffic prospects. I had written ahead and was jubilant when Curran approved my plan to rent a steam train. Whitaker and Jensen arrived from New York and, true to his word, Mr. Curran had Columbkille fired up and a train of coaches including Donegal's ancient but excellent six wheel private car. Curran told us that a long list of notables including Queen Victoria had used the private car on previous occasions. Whitaker observed that this was akin to the legends surrounding all the rooms in which George Washington had allegedly slept. There are more rooms than nights in George Washington's lifetime, he declared.

At Killybegs, our engine cut off and ran to a turntable, took on water and then waited at the tank while we lunched at a recommended pub. Whitaker was affecting a black bowler hat and as he entered the pub, the publican looked up and spontaneously asked, "What will it be, my lord?". Whitaker took this completely in his stride as he ordered a gin and lime to accompany a sandwich. And truth to tell, the bowler hat thereafter became a Whitaker trademark.

Our trip to the marvelous Donegal Railways brought back more than a memory. It also brought home a complete Irish narrow gauge train. An hour's drive north of Ennis brought me to the country village of Ballinamore, County Leitrim, "in the midst of the bog," as they told me. On the east side I came across the station, yard, shops and engine house of the Cavan and Leitrim line. For the opening of the line came eight identical 4-4-0T engines from Robert Stephenson & Son at Newcastle-upon-Tyne in England. The engines were fast, powerful and popular, and most of them lasted until final closure in April 1959.

Even the Leitrim mainline was full of hills, but there was one long, straight stretch on the upper section where engineers opened the throttle very wide to make up time. I was told that Class 3L Lady Edith had easily made 60 mph on several occasions. In fact, it was common knowledge that No. 3L

was an excellent engine in every way. For one matter it had a new boiler and had been through an extensive overhaul at Inchicore Shops near Dublin a year or so before.

I had wired ahead that I expected to be in Ballinamore, a habit which has reaped dividends in the past. In this case, Robert D. Martin, District Locomotive Supervisor, made it a point to be in town. I was slightly taken aback by the presence of an official but decided to seize the opportunity of acting out the part of an American tourist interested in quaint railways. I invited him to lunch at the main pub in town.

I asked Martin if any of the engines and cars might possibly be for sale. Not only could they be bought for preservation, he said, but they could be bought quite cheaply, and the company would co-operate in moving these purchases to Longwall docks near Dublin. Since No. 3L had received replacement boiler, firebox, wheel tires and bearings and had received classified repairs in 1947, 1956 and 1959, a price was to be established for No. 3L, and even a timetable for shipment agreed upon. Martin would have the boiler hydrostatically tested to 240 pounds and it subsequently passed without difficulty. When I caught up with Whitaker and Jensen at Stranorlar, I explained my impromptu plan to bring old Lady Edith to America, and they soon agreed to become partners in this insane venture. A Tralee and Dingle first class coach was to be imported to keep 'The Lady' company in a strange land. The coach had green cushions and scenes of County Kerry in frames on the walls.

It would be tedious to discuss the volume of correspondence, telegrams, telephone calls, field trips and general paperwork involved in transporting this equipment from Ireland to the United States. Shipping Agents, customs agents, and lighterage companies mailed out forms in nothing less than triplicate. Invoices flew, all in our direction. The engine was loaded at Dromod by a broad gauge steam crane, taken to Dublin and then lifted aboard United States Line's American Press for a deck cargo journey to Boston. Tralee and Dingle coach No. 21 also made the trip. Dock hands scribbled 'Remember Ireland' in chalk on the sides and added a shamrock. When American Press put into Glasgow to take on a cargo of whiskey, Scottish dockhands, not to be outdone, wrote 'Remember Scotland' on the other side and drew a large thistle. The little train arrived at Boston on July 8, 1959 and went on display at Wakefield, Massachusetts for a few years before moving to New Jersey Museum of Transportation at Allaire Park.

The Irish steam engine created quite a dilemma for the New Jersey boiler inspectors. By slow steps, however, the State Commissioners came 'on board' and passed the boiler for operation. The engine soon found its niche in Pine Creek Museum train operations.'

13
THE LADY EDITH SOCIETY

EDGAR T. MEAD

A commerical postcard of *Lady Edith* hauling two Tralee & Dingle carriages at the New Jersey Museum of Transport in Maine, USA.

Of course, there are very many Irish people now living in the United States. A huge number of them emigrated in the search for a better life. Many were even paid the princely sum of £5 to do so, with their passage also found by English landlords, who wanted to break the feudal agricultural system whereby parcels of land were continually split into smaller pieces when passed on to the next generation. Nowadays, millions of subsequent generations return to Eire to see the land of their forefathers, Dingle being an especially popular destination and one where the rehabilitation of a famous 3ft narrow gauge system, the Tralee & Dingle, would not go amiss.

However, the tale in this essay relates to some extraordinary Americans who spent much time hunting steam locomotives. Rogers E.M. 'Frimbo' Whitaker was the Editor of the *New Yorker* and full of dry humour. He wrote about his quest to honour the steam locomotive when visiting 'the Red Baron', an Austrian friend:

'We are big game hunters of the chase, deferring to none in our fondness for the steam locomotive, that herald and forerunner of a civilization that now appears bent upon the destruction of its great benefactor. It is our purpose, in our role as hunters, to seek out like objects of our veneration – not to destroy but to enhance, not to confine but to set free, to let them roam the countryside of which they were once king. The relationships between man and his cat, man and his dog, man and his steam locomotive are supernal ones – matches made in Heaven – and their justification is the supreme delight they engender. It is within reason to suspect that veneration of the steam locomotive is the finest pleasure on earth. This pleasure lies not in the worship of a graven image; it lies in the worship of a creature as full of life and energy and ambition and bluster as we ourselves are.'

Whitaker journeyed to Ireland in the company of Oliver O. Jensen, editor of *American Heritage* magazine, and Edgar T. Mead – Americans always use all of their initials!